AN ALBUM OF MODERN SPACESHIPS

AN ALBUM OF
MODERN SPACESHIPS

BY GREGORY VOGT

A GROLIER COMPANY

FRANKLIN WATTS
NEW YORK/LONDON/TORONTO/SYDNEY/1987

Illustration on p. 11 (right) courtesy of
Across the Space Frontier,
Cornelius Ryan, editor, Viking Press, 1952.

All photographs courtesy of NASA except: UPI/Bettmann
Newsphotos: p. 11 (bottom left); Lockheed: p. 29 (Dave Scholl);
British Aerospace PLC: p. 83; MBB-ERNO: p. 84.

Library of Congress Cataloging-in-Publication Data

Vogt, Gregory.
An album of modern spaceships.

Includes index.
Summary: An illustrated history of developments in
manned spaceships, including a discussion of future
programs and the effect of the "Challenger" tragedy.
1. Astronautics—Juvenile literature.
2. Manned space flight—Juvenile literature.
[1. Astronautics. 2. Manned space flight.
3. Space vehicles] I. Title.
TL793.V55   1987   629.47   87-10722
ISBN 0-531-10397-8

CONTENTS

*This book is dedicated
in fond appreciation to my
dear friend, uncle-in-law,
and photography mentor
Eugene Hollander.*

1

ACROSS THE SPACE FRONTIER

Within the next ten or fifteen years, the earth can have a new companion in the skies, a man-made satellite which will be man's first foothold in space. Inhabited by human beings, and visible from the ground as a sedately moving star, it will sweep around the earth at an incredible rate of speed in that dark void beyond the atmosphere which is known as "space."

Werner von Braun
1952

Werner von Braun was a scientist who dreamed of space travel. As a young man, his accomplishments in rocketry had gained him notice, and he soon found himself leading the German effort that produced the devastating V2 rocket missile near the end of World War II. At war's end he joined the fledgling U.S. space program and was instrumental in the design of the rocket that made it possible for American astronauts to walk on the Moon. Though he worked for a time on weapons making, von Braun's dream was first and always the exploration of outer space.

In 1952, before any humans had reached outer space and five years before the first artificial satellite went into orbit, von Braun discussed his dream of space exploration in a book entitled *Across the Space Frontier*. He envisioned a large,

[9]

An early space station design based on the von Braun concept

wheel-shaped space station in which humans would orbit the Earth every two hours. From the station manned expeditions to the Moon and later to Mars would be launched. The station was something that could be accomplished for a sum of $4 billion over a period of ten to fifteen years. But to make the dream possible required a "winged spaceship" able to carry up the space-station segments.

Considering that the world was just learning about space flight by launching unused German V2 missiles, von Braun's dream seemed, to put it mildly, far-fetched. The "winged spaceship" to make the space station all happen was itself a major challenge. As von Braun envisioned it, it would stand 265 feet (81 m) tall, have a 65-foot-diameter (20 m) base, and weigh 7,000 tons. At lift-off, fifty-one rocket motors burning hydrazine (similar to ammonia) and nitric acid propellants would generate 14,000 tons of thrust. Twenty-five miles (40 km) above the launch site the first stage would drop off and parachute to the ocean. The second stage would then fire, carrying the vehicle higher, then fall back also. Lastly, the five engines in the tail of the winged spaceship would make the final push for orbit.

Von Braun's design for a winged spaceship featured a cone-shaped body with small wings on its nose and huge wings with a 156-foot (48-m) span toward the rear. It would be capable of carrying a crew and 36.5 tons of cargo to the space-station site. When a mission was completed, the winged spaceship would fire braking rockets, causing it to fall out of orbit. The ship's nearly 4,000 square feet (372 sq m) of wing surface would catch the thin upper atmosphere and begin a long, airplanelike glide. Glowing red from friction with the air, the winged spaceship would descend through denser and denser air, finally slowing to a mere 65 miles per hour (105 kph) as its landing gear touched the runway only a short distance from its rocket-launch site of a few days before. Following refurbishment, the winged spaceship would be hoisted atop the recovered first and second stages of the booster and be readied for another launch.

Von Braun's 1952 design for a winged spaceship never traveled beyond the drawing-board stage. The urgency of being the first nation to reach space caused both the United States and the Soviet Union to choose simpler, faster, and less costly means of sending humans into orbit. The Soviets did it first when they launched Yuri Gagarin on April 12, 1961, for a single-orbit flight of the Earth. "Man's first foothold in space" came within the ten- to fifteen-year time frame von Braun predicted, but the 5-ton expendable Vostok spacecraft Gagarin rode in was a far cry from the majestic reusable winged spaceship von Braun had envisioned.

For the next twenty years, every astronaut and cosmonaut who traveled to space did so on the top of an expendable, or throwaway, rocket. There were

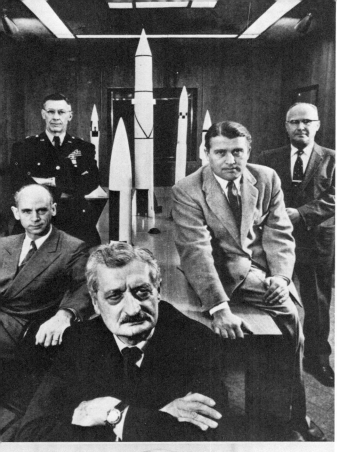

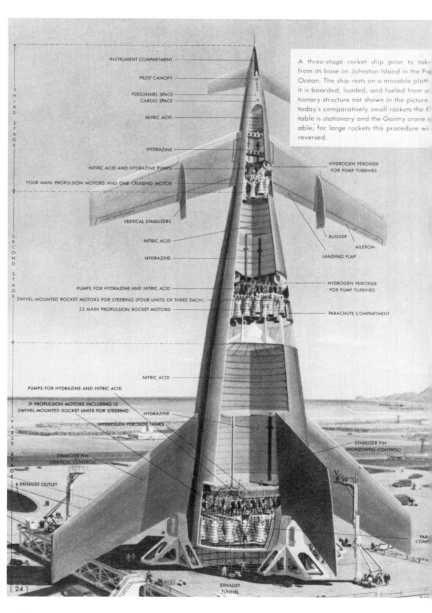

Top left: *Werner von Braun (seated on table) is pictured with his colleagues at the Army Ballistic Missile Agency in Huntsville, Alabama, in 1956.* Bottom left: *Yuri Gagarin becomes the first human to travel in space.* Right: *Von Braun's winged spaceship stands on the launch pad in this artist's cutaway drawing of his concept.*

spacecraft rendezvous and linkups, spacewalks, small space stations, retrieval and repair of satellites, and walks on the Moon but no winged spaceship. It was much more difficult and expensive to build than von Braun had predicted. Nevertheless, the idea did not die. On April 12, 1981, exactly twenty years after Gagarin's historic flight and nearly four years after Werner von Braun's own death, his dream finally came true. *Columbia*, the world's first reusable winged spaceship, rocketed off to outer space.

The first flight of the space shuttle now seems long ago. Much has happened since then, including the tragic loss of the space shuttle *Challenger* and its crew of seven. The loss grounded the entire space shuttle fleet for safety redesign but did little to dampen worldwide enthusiasm for the development of other types of winged spaceships. Work is proceeding in the Soviet Union today on the building and testing of two shuttlelike vehicles. The European Space Agency (ESA) has started planning work on *Hermes*, a spaceplane. Japan has been conducting wind tunnel and drop tests on alternate designs of a possible small space shuttle of its own. The United States, United Kingdom, and West Germany are each looking at new winged spaceships for the twenty-first century that will take off like airplanes from airport runways and soar into space. Although expendable rockets will still be used for launching artificial satellites and space probes for a long time to come, it is clear that for the remainder of this century and for the first few decades beyond, the future of space travel will belong to Werner von Braun's winged spaceships.

Top left: Apollo 11 *heads for the Moon, signaling the start of man's first lunar mission.* **Top right:** *Apollo 11 astronaut Edward "Buzz" Aldrin, Jr., climbs down the ladder for a walk on the Moon.* **Below:** *the space shuttle* Columbia *rockets off for the first space test of a winged spaceship.*

[13]

2

THE NEED FOR
THE SPACE SHUTTLE

Each time the National Aeronautics and Space Administration (NASA) launched a team of astronauts to the Moon, a tremendous amount of space hardware was discarded. The huge 365-foot-tall (111 m) Saturn V rocket was capable of the Moon trip only by dropping off its segments along the way. The first stage, burning rocket propellants at a rate of 2,230 gallons (8,440 liters) per second, or a total 4.6 million pounds (2.1 million kg) of propellants in the 160 seconds the stage operated, was exhausted at 41 miles (66 km) and dropped back to the ocean. The second stage dropped off at 116 miles (186 km), and it, too, fell back. Both the first and second stages were destroyed by their return. The third stage propelled the lander onto the Moon but was then sent into solar orbit or aimed at the Moon to crash and cause vibrations that would be recorded by scientific instruments left by earlier missions. After the Moon walks, the lower half of the lander was left on the Moon while the upper half carried the crew to a rendezvous in lunar orbit with the main spacecraft. The remainder of the lander was then abandoned also. By the time the astronauts splashed down in the Pacific Ocean, all that was left of the rocket was an 11-foot-high (3.4 m) capsule. At a cost of more than $100 million per Saturn V rocket, travel to the Moon was an expensive proposition.

In April of 1972, *Apollo 16* astronaut John Young was on a lunar rock-collecting trip. Because of the low lunar gravity, he was able to bound from place to place on the Moon in spite of his bulky space suit. While tending to

Left: *the giant "throwaway" Saturn V rocket sends the Apollo 11 crew on their way to the Moon.* **Below:** *an Apollo space capsule splashes down in the Pacific Ocean following atmospheric reentry.*

business, he received a radio call from Earth telling him that the United States had approved a program that would replace the Saturn V rocket with a reusable winged spaceship—the space shuttle. John Young didn't know it at the time, but nine years later, he would be the first to command a space shuttle mission.

Building a reusable winged spaceship was no simple task. It would have to stand up on its tail and blast off into space as a rocket, orbit the Earth as a spacecraft, and survive reentry into the Earth's atmosphere so that it could glide down to a runway like an airplane. Furthermore, the proposed vehicle would have to be able to carry a large payload to orbit and even be able to return some of it to Earth. To make things even more difficult, the orbital vehicle would have to be reusable for a hundred or more flights. All these criteria, it was felt, would make the space shuttle much more versatile than the Saturn V rocket and certainly cheaper to operate. With the main details identified and approved by Congress, NASA set out to test its concept and begin construction.

Like every rocket before, the space shuttle would have to be built in stages. Reaching space took tremendous amounts of propellants and very heavy tanks to hold them. Large energy savings could be made by dropping empty propellant tanks when they were no longer needed.

NASA examined a number of proposed space shuttle designs before settling on the final design. Some of the designs called for a sophisticated hybrid engine capable of acting as a jet in the atmosphere and as a rocket in space. This could mean that both jet and rocket fuel would have to be carried as well as a liquid-oxygen supply for use in space. Another design placed dual engines on the orbiter—one set of rocket engines in the tail for use in space and one set of retractable turbofan jet engines on its upper surface for use in the atmosphere. Several plans proposed using a large winged first stage that would ferry the winged spaceship to an altitude above Earth high enough for the spaceship to be able to continue up into orbit on its own. After using up its propellants, the first stage would be flown back to a landing strip by the pilot on board. A much simpler alternative to this was an expendable booster that could be replaced after each flight.

To help in the decision-making process, NASA drew upon years of atmospheric and space flight research. It had been conducting design studies of the space shuttle concept for years. One important research program had

Early space shuttle concepts often included a winged first stage that returned to a runway following the boost phase of the mission.

begun in the early 1960s. It was a program to flight-test wingless aircraft called *lifting bodies*. Lifting bodies were built in the shape of half a cone, when the cone has been sliced in half the long way. The purpose of the tests was to learn about the dynamics of orbital reentry vehicle designs that permitted controlled gliding flight and maneuvering on the way down. With the exception of a few rocket-launched tests, most lifting-body flights were conducted entirely in the atmosphere. The lifting body was carried high above the California desert, the site of the NASA Flight Research Center (now called the Dryden Flight Research Facility), while slung underneath the wing of a B-52 carrier aircraft. When the proper altitude was reached, it was dropped to the desert below. On the way down, the pilot on board conducted various control tests while gliding at frighteningly high speeds and steep angles to a dirt landing strip below. In some tests, the lifting body pilots fired onboard rocket engines after being dropped, to learn more about the ship's handling characteristics.

In one particularly terrifying test, Bruce Peterson was piloting the M2F2 lifting body toward a landing when a helicopter near the ground got in his way. Although he was able to maneuver to avoid a collision, one of the doors that open when the landing gear pop out caught the ground, causing the vehicle to flip. The wingless, somewhat rounded lifting body seemed to bound, tumble, and scrape endlessly on the desert floor, kicking up billowing clouds of dust before it finally came to a stop. Miraculously Bruce Peterson survived. Later, films of the crash were borrowed by Hollywood television producers, and Peterson's lifting-body crash became the inspiration for the *Six Million Dollar Man* TV show.

The designs needed for the new space shuttle were many, and teams of government and industry scientists, engineers, and administrators proposed their various ideas forth and back until an agreement was reached. In the end, the simplest plan was adopted. It would be a four-part rocket.

The space shuttle would consist first of the *orbiter*, a delta- or triangular-winged reusable orbital spaceship. For launch, the orbiter would stand on its tail and be mounted to the side of a large external propellant tank (ET). The tank would hold millions of gallons of liquid hydrogen and oxygen but would

Above: *the X-24B lifting body makes its final powered test flight.* **Below**: *Three lifting body aircraft sit next to each other on a desert lakebed. They are (left to right) the X-24A, the M-2, and the HL-10.*

Wind tunnel test of a miniature model of the space shuttle

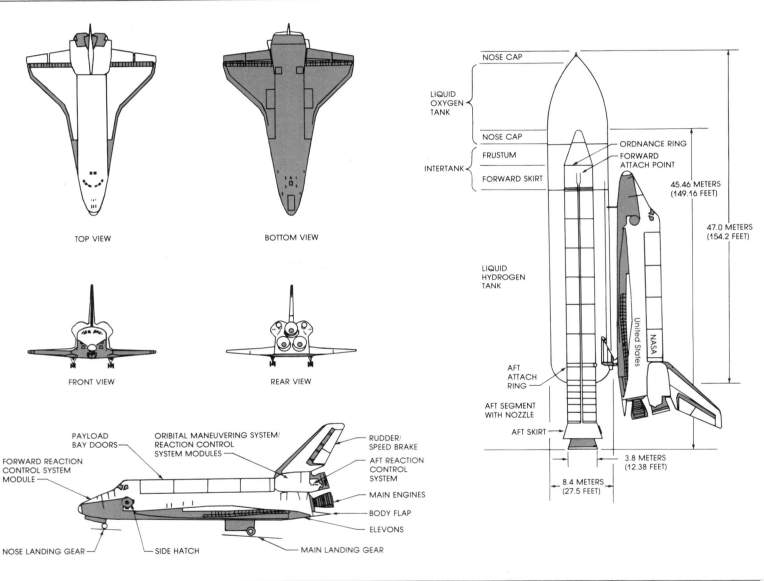

TOP VIEW

BOTTOM VIEW

FRONT VIEW

REAR VIEW

NOSE CAP

LIQUID OXYGEN TANK

NOSE CAP

FRUSTUM

INTERTANK

FORWARD SKIRT

ORDNANCE RING

FORWARD ATTACH POINT

45.46 METERS (149.16 FEET)

47.0 METERS (154.2 FEET)

LIQUID HYDROGEN TANK

United States

NASA

AFT ATTACH RING

AFT SEGMENT WITH NOZZLE

AFT SKIRT

3.8 METERS (12.38 FEET)

8.4 METERS (27.5 FEET)

PAYLOAD BAY DOORS

ORIBITAL MANEUVERING SYSTEM/ REACTION CONTROL SYSTEM MODULES

RUDDER/ SPEED BRAKE

FORWARD REACTION CONTROL SYSTEM MODULE

AFT REACTION CONTROL SYSTEM

MAIN ENGINES

BODY FLAP

ELEVONS

NOSE LANDING GEAR

SIDE HATCH

MAIN LANDING GEAR

contain no engines for its propellants. The main engines along with propellant suction pumps would be mounted in the orbiter's tail. This meant that the external tank could be expendable because all of the really expensive engine and plumbing components would be recovered with the orbiter. Using an expendable external tank would be much simpler and less costly in the short run than building a recoverable tank that would fly back to Earth as in earlier plans.

The remaining two parts of the space shuttle were a pair of solid rocket boosters (SRBs) that would be strapped to opposite sides of the external tank. The solid rocket boosters would provide the largest share of the liftoff thrust but become exhausted in only two minutes. Each booster would carry parachutes for soft landing in the ocean down range from the launch site for recovery by ship and be usable for an additional nineteen or more flights. Using solid rocket boosters for a space launch with people aboard was something that had never been done before. However, solid rocket booster technology was relatively simple compared to the technology of liquid-propellant rocket engines and therefore was considered less likely to cause major problems.

The final design of the space shuttle included a reusable orbiter, solid rocket boosters, and an expendable external tank

3

BUILDING
THE SHUTTLE

As with every other NASA rocket, the building of the space shuttle would be done primarily by American industry. Rockwell International won the contract to build the orbiter. Martin Marietta would build the external tank, and Morton Thiokol was selected for the solid rocket boosters. Each of the prime contractors, in turn, subcontracted smaller pieces of their work to other companies so that in the end, many thousands of workers over virtually the entire United States had some hand in building the space shuttle.

Meanwhile, NASA itself was refining its own program. As a further cost savings, existing Saturn V launch hardware was adapted to shuttle use. The majority of all shuttle launches would take place at the Kennedy Space Center in Florida, although plans were also laid for a second launch facility at Vandenburg Air Force Base in Lompoc, California. Both sides were situated on ocean shorelines primarily for safety reasons. Any rocket experiencing a malfunction requiring a self-destruct order would rain debris down on the ocean rather than on populated areas. The Kennedy Space Center was ideally suited for mid-latitude launches (orbits that cover the mid-latitude regions of Earth). The Vandenburg site was most suited for high-latitude and polar-orbiting flights. To achieve a polar orbit, the shuttle must take off on a due north or a due south heading. In north and south launches from the Kennedy Space Center, the vehicle would have to pass over populated areas before reaching orbit, therefore making those launches especially dangerous. At Vandenburg, shuttles

Top left: *construction of the space shuttle air frame at the Rockwell assembly plant in California.* Top right: *the framework for the liquid oxygen portion of the external tank is being hoisted at the Martin Marietta assembly facility.* Bottom: *a completed external tank is being moved into the vehicle assembly building at the Kennedy Space Center.*

Right: *a water tower that holds 300,000 gallons (1.14 million liters) of water for spraying on the launch pad at Kennedy Space Center to reduce sound during a launch stands in the foreground. Far right: doors are being installed in the rotation service structure on the shuttle launch pad.*

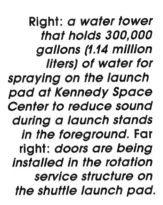

The 15,000-foot (4,600-m) -long orbiter runway is visible off in the distance beyond the vehicle assembly building.

can take off due south, and the first land encountered in that direction is Antarctica.

At the Kennedy Space Center, the same launch pads that were used for Saturn V rockets could also be used for the shuttle. The mobile launch pad was modified by the removal of the tall gantry (supporting structure) from its upper section. A new launch support structure was permanently installed in its place on the launch pad. Part of that structure, the rotating service structure, swings into position to surround much of the shuttle while it is being prepared for flight.

Kennedy's Launch Control Center was also modified primarily by the removal of many counsel stations for launch controllers. During a Saturn V launch, as many as 450 technicians sat at monitoring stations to supervise the launch. For the shuttle, upgraded computerization reduced the number of controllers to approximately forty-five—one-tenth as many as used for an Apollo launch.

One additional major modification of the shuttle launch site was necessary. The orbiter was going to glide back to Earth and land on a runway. A 15,000-foot-long, 300-foot-wide (4,572 m by 91 m) runway was constructed a few miles northwest of the vehicle assembly building (VAB). The building was originally built to assemble Saturn V rockets upright on their mobile launch pads. It would be used the same way for the shuttle. After payloads were inserted into the orbiter's payload bay in a small orbiter processor facility building nearby, the orbiter would be brought into the VAB for assembly with the external tank and boosters. From there, it would be rolled out to the pad, launched into space, come back down on the runway, and be brought back into the VAB for refurbishment and reassembly in preparation for its next rollout and flight.

APPROACH AND LANDING TESTS

As the time for the first space shuttle flight neared, all shuttle components had to be thoroughly tested. The SRBs were laid on their side and anchored to the Utah desert floor near their assembly plant for test firings. The external tank was put through torturous vibration tests, checking for structural faults that might appear during the stress of an actual launch. The main engines of the orbiter were tested and retested. When ready for flight, they would be the most powerful liquid oxygen and hydrogen engines ever built. That criterion alone caused problems, and many engines failed or even exploded as engine testers pushed their state-of-the-art designs to the limits. Setbacks in engine and other test programs began to push back the first launch date.

Another very important series of tests was to be performed on the orbiter. The first orbiter constructed was a test model, and it rolled out for public viewing from its assembly plant in California on September 17, 1976. It was named the

Enterprise after an old sailing ship. The name pleased the ardent fans of the *Star Trek* television show, where the principal spaceship also had the same name. Some of the actors in the show were on hand to greet the space shuttle *Enterprise* during its unveiling.

Months later, in 1977, the *Enterprise* was hoisted on top of a specially modified Boeing 747 aircraft for a series of approach and landing tests. Although orbiter designs were tested countless times with wind-tunnel model and computer simulations, before any shuttle would fly in space it would also have to be tested under actual flight conditions that could simulate a landing from space. Hence, the 747.

With two astronauts inside riding on the flight deck (cockpit) to pilot the *Enterprise* down, the 747 climbed high above the same desert floor used for lifting-body tests years before. At the agreed-upon moment, when the 747 and its piggyback cargo were down range of the landing strip, the aircraft was piloted into a shallow dive. The *Enterprise* astronauts fired explosive bolts to break contact with the 747, and the shuttle became airborne on its own. Though the test goal was simple—to glide the craft down to a safe landing—bringing it off successfully was another matter. The fact that the shuttle had to make a landing without engine power and had a relatively small wing surface in relation to its weight caused it to have all the flight characteristics of what the astronauts jokingly termed a "well-designed brick." The key to landing was speed. As long as the runway approach angle was about six to eight times steeper than the angle used by commercial jetliners, the orbiter would maintain its speed through falling so that it would glide and give the astronauts the needed aerodynamic control. For much of the way down, the *Enterprise*'s speed was maintained at 270 knots, but near the ground the nose was pitched up so that the craft's nearly flat undersurface could catch the air and slow the *Enterprise* to a landing speed of about 175 knots. A much slower speed would cause the *Enterprise* to stall and fall like a real brick.

The approach and landing test series was originally planned to consist of eight free flights. During the first four flights the *Enterprise* was successfully dropped from elevations ranging from 18,000 to 24,000 feet (5,500 to 7,300 m). The tests were so successful that NASA management decided that the remaining four tests were unnecessary and canceled them.

Following the flight tests, the *Enterprise* was sent off on a variety of missions while its sister orbiter, the *Columbia*, the first space shuttle scheduled to fly in space, was undergoing finishing touches at its California assembly plant. The *Enterprise* was sent to the Marshall Space Flight Center in Alabama for vibration tests and to the Kennedy Space Center for practice in attaching it to the external fuel tank and boosters and for checkout with the mobile launcher and launch support structures.

Left: *"Star Trek" crew members are on hand for the rollout of the shuttle orbiter* Enterprise *on September 17, 1976. Left to right: NASA Administrator James Fletcher, DeForest Kelley (Dr. McCoy), George Taki (Mr. Sulu), Michelle Nichols (Lt. Uhura), Leonard Nimoy (Mr. Spock), Gene Roddenberry ("Star Trek" producer), and Walter Koenig (Ens. Chekhov). Below: The shuttle orbiter* Enterprise *separates from the carrier aircraft on an approach and landing test.*

THERMAL PROTECTION TROUBLES

For the space shuttle orbiter to be truly reusable, it had to have a reusable thermal (heat) protection system. Returning to Earth from space involves passing through a torturous period of atmospheric friction, where surface temperatures of the reentry vehicle can reach 3,000°F (1,650°C) or more. No known materials could survive such temperatures and friction. Previously, all spacecraft with people aboard had used the "meteorite principle" for reentry. When a meteorite enters the atmosphere, its outer surface vaporizes in the high heat generated. The steaming vapor simply carries away the heat, leaving the inner material relatively cool. The process is called *ablative cooling*. Spacecraft heat shields were therefore designed to burn off and by so doing, carry away the heat. Unfortunately, the shield was destroyed with just one reentry.

The space shuttle orbiter, being as large as a DC-9 jet, was simply too big to allow for its heat shield to be entirely replaced after every flight. The alternative was a shield made of materials that could survive reentry. In tests it was learned that different areas of the orbiter's exterior would receive different amounts of reentry heat. This permitted shuttle designers to custom-design the heat shield to meet the various demands. The areas of highest heating—the nose and leading edges of the wings—were protected with a heavy new material called *reinforced carbon-carbon*. Most of the orbiter's underside and much of its topside could be protected with a lightweight silicon-fiber material that was coated with ceramic. The material was cut into blocks averaging about 6 inches (15 cm) square and glued to the outside surface. Tiles on the top were coated white and tiles on the bottom were coated black.

Putting together the heat shield on the *Columbia* turned out to be a nightmarish task. Nearly 32,000 tiles, each one of them different, were needed to cover the orbiter, and each one had to be hand-applied. The process was exacting, and many hours were needed for placing each tile. Getting the tiles in place and keeping them there took longer than thought, contributing to additional delays in the first launch.

FAILED RESCUE

The prospect of additional delays in the first launch caused Congress and the news media to put pressure on NASA to get on with the task. Part of the problem was due to underfunding of the shuttle program by Congress, which also meant that NASA had to reduce spending in other areas of research to keep the shuttle going. Planetary research scientists were especially dismayed when NASA announced it would not fund a space-probe mission to Halley's Comet. Further pressure came quite literally from the Sun.

Some of the thousands of unique shapes used
for thermal protection tiles. A technician's
picture showing him holding a red-hot piece
of tile is superimposed on the nearest tile.

*The Skylab space station orbit eventually decayed,
and the station was destroyed before a shuttle
rescue mission could be launched.*

In 1973 the last of the Saturn V rockets to fly carried the *Skylab* space station to a 270-mile-high (435 km) orbit. By the end of the mission three teams of American astronauts had successfully spent a total of 168 days on board. *Skylab*, a valuable orbital laboratory, then remained vacant for five years. Although thought to have been placed in a stable orbit that would last many years, *Skylab* actually started a slow fall. Increased solar activity was causing a warming and consequent expansion of the Earth's upper atmosphere. Molecules of air began dragging on the space station, causing it to slow and to begin orbital decay.

Although the exact date of *Skylab*'s demise was difficult to predict, there was a chance that the *Columbia* might be ready in time to carry up a rescue system on its first flight. The system was a teleoperated, or remote-controlled, rocket booster. In other words, it was a package that would be ejected by *Columbia*, fly up to *Skylab*, attach itself, and fire a rocket booster to raise the station to a safe orbit.

Unfortunately, continued launch delays and a faster than expected deceleration of the space station prevented the rescue attempt. *Skylab* became a fireball over the Indian Ocean west of Australia in early July 1979.

GETTING THE CREW READY

At best, even without the delays, the first launch of the space shuttle would have meant a four-year gap in American space flights with people aboard. The last such flight was the 1975 combined American and Soviet Apollo–Soyuz mission. With the delays, the gap began to widen.

During the down time, many of the older veteran astronauts retired from flight status and went on to other careers. NASA's ambitious plans, calling for up to one shuttle flight per week in some years, meant that many new and younger astronauts would be needed to fill the heavy schedule. The call for shuttle astronauts brought more than 8,000 applicants, who were finally reduced to thirty-five when the selections were announced. Most notable among the selections were NASA's first six female astronauts.

In the beginning, the thirty-five astronauts were officially called "astronaut candidates." They would be put through a year of training and evaluation to make sure they were suitable for NASA. Training meant many things, including being assigned to a "big brother" veteran astronaut to learn the ropes. Hundreds of hours were spent in classrooms, poring over operations manuals; in flight training in high-performance jet aircraft; and in taking parachute and water-survival training. In one especially memorable activity, the candidates climbed aboard a commercial-size jetliner with most of its seats removed and its interior walls covered with padding. The plane took off, climbed to a high altitude, and began a series of dives that made the astronaut candidates inside weightless. For periods of as long as thirty seconds, they could feel what weightlessness was like. For some candidates, the repeated up, down, and pullout motions caused nausea, a problem that earned the plane the nickname of "Vomit Comet."

In the end all the candidates passed muster and were promoted to flight status. Each was assigned an area of specialty, such as piloting the orbiter, working payloads, developing food-handling systems, and satellite deployment. Astronauts who would pilot the orbiter were simply called pilot astronauts, and those who would concentrate on the experiments and payloads of various missions were called mission specialists.

Special training facilities were set up to simulate flight conditions. This was a tradition begun in the days of the first manned space flights. It was started with the belief that orbiting the Earth in a space capsule is not the best time to find out you really don't know how to fly the thing. Simulators were designed to reproduce as many of the actual flight conditions as possible. Pilot astronauts rehearsed lift-off, orbital operations, and reentry and landing on board the "1 G Trainer" at the Johnson Space Center in Houston, Texas. The trainer was set up to be an exact replica of the nose of a shuttle orbiter, with all the proper controls and hardware found in the upper flight deck and the lower middeck of the crew cabin. The controls were tied into a computer that simulated actual flight-instrument readings and responded to control commands of the crew. The only really significant difference of the 1 G Trainer from actual space flight was that it remained on the ground during the entire mission.

While pilot astronauts were on the flight deck of the 1 G Trainer, mission specialists might be on the middeck practicing meal preparation, unstowing experimental apparatus, running practice experiments, or even trying on space suit parts. In another simulator nearby, simulating the aft (rear) portion of the flight deck and the orbiter's payload bay, a mission specialist might be practicing with the controls for the remote manipulator system (RMS) arm. The RMS

Above: *NASA's first six women astronauts: Left to right, Rhea Seddon, Sally K. Ride (the first American woman to fly in space), Kathryn Sullivan, Shannon Lucid, Anna L. Fisher, and Judith A. Resnick (later killed in the* Challenger *explosion).* **Below:** *astronaut candidates feel what weightlessness is like aboard the "Vomit Comet."*

is a 50-foot-long (15-m) mechanical arm with "shoulder," "elbow," and "wrist" for bending and reaching into the payload bay. An "end effector," or wire snare device for hooking onto payloads, is located at the end of the arm. By careful manipulation of the arm, simulated payloads could be plucked out of the bay, maneuvered in the air, and brought back in.

In another facility nearby, other mission specialists might be donning specially equipped space suits and stepping into a large swimming pool that contained a replica of an entire orbiter payload bay. The suits were weighted to make them just heavy enough so that they wouldn't sink or float. In other words, they were neutrally buoyant, a condition very similar to weightlessness in space. With safety technicians wearing normal diving equipment and swimming nearby, the space-suited mission specialists would rehearse various extravehicular tasks.

Above: *a 1 G version of the orbiter's Remote Manipulator System arm enables mission specialists to learn how to manipulate cargo in the payload bay.* **Below left:** *Donald Williams and Rhea Seddon practice space meal preparation techniques.* **Below right:** *Anna Fisher prepares to practice spacewalking underwater.*

4

THE *COLUMBIA*

All the years of development, including the frustrations, delays, and technological leaps, finally came together on the morning of April 12, 1981. The space shuttle *Columbia* sat upright on the launch pad in the early morning hours. On board was a crew of two. Sitting in the left seat was commander John Young, veteran of four space flights, including a walk on the Moon. In the right seat sat pilot and space rookie Robert Crippen. The two had been set to take the *Columbia* up on its first space flight two days earlier, but onboard computer timing problems caused cancellation of the liftoff. The second attempt was coincidentally twenty years to the day after Yuri Gagarin ushered in the new age of human space flight. *Columbia* would usher in its own new age, that of reusable spaceships.

At 7:00 A.M. eastern standard time, *Columbia*'s three main engines and the two solid rocket boosters came to life. Rising slowly at first and then picking up speed, the vehicle streaked skyward on a pillar of fire and smoke. It was the first time all space shuttle components were assembled and operated together, and all worked virtually without flaw.

On board, Crippen exclaimed "Man, that was one fantastic ride," while his heartbeat rate rose from 60 to 130 beats per minute. The heartbeat of the fifty-year-old space veteran Commander Young rose only from 60 to 85. He later explained that he was excited, too: "But I just can't make it go any faster," he said.

[36]

The space shuttle Columbia *lifts off on its historic first flight at 7 a.m. EST on April 12, 1981.*

Once in orbit, Young and Crippen set about evaluating the condition of their orbiter. An early task was the opening of the payload bay doors. Although 10,823 pounds (4,970 kg) of flight-evaluation instruments were sitting in the bay, no actual payload was carried inside. Opening the doors was important mainly for heat control. Large metal radiators, fitted inside the doors, were exposed to space, and they began radiating away accumulated heat from the Sun and from the electronic equipment in the cabin. When the doors were opened, the crew called down to Mission Control that some sixteen of the thousands of heat-shield tiles covering the outside of the orbiter were lost or chipped. These were on the curved upper surface and covered the orbital maneuvering system engine pods near the vertical tail. Immediately, mission controllers began to wonder if other tiles were lost on the more critical lower surface where the crew could not see. There would be no way to know for sure until the vehicle began its reentry.

About two days and four hours after liftoff, *Columbia* was turned around and its orbital maneuvering engines were fired, producing a braking effect. Diminishing its 17,500 mile per hour (28,000 kmph) velocity by just a few hundred feet per second was enough to start the long fall back to Earth. With its nose pitched up at about 40° so that its underside could take the brunt of atmospheric friction, *Columbia* slammed into the atmosphere high above the western Pacific Ocean. From there on, its fall was a steep glide until it touched the runway on Roger's Dry Lake in the Mojave Desert of California just seconds under fifty-four hours and twenty minutes after liftoff. The crew and *Columbia* were safe, and the first chapter in a new era in space transportation had just closed.

Over the next fifteen months, *Columbia* made three more test flights. Each of the shuttle flights was designated with the initials "STS" followed by a number. The initials stood for Space Transportation System and the number for the order of the flight. (Following STS-9, the numbering system was changed to two numbers followed by a letter. The first number indicated the fiscal year in which the flight was assigned to fly. The second number indicated the launch site; a 1 meant the Kennedy Space Center and a 2 meant the Vandenburg site. The letter indicated the order of the flight for that year. In practice, scheduling changes sometimes rearranged the flight orders even though the letters remained the same.) Like STS-1, STS-2 to STS-4 each carried two crew members. The flight-evaluation instrument package was replaced with increasingly heavy scientific payloads that studied the Earth and its near-space environment. By the time of STS-4, the payload weight reached 24,492 pounds (11,021 kg).

The landing of Columbia following its fourth successful flight on July 4, 1982, closed the second chapter of the new era. The test-flight series was completed, and in spite of the early return of *Columbia* on STS-2 because of fuel-cell

Left: *with payload bay doors open, the STS-1 crew notes the loss and damage of several thermal tiles on the curved surfaces of the OMS engine pods to the right and left of the tail.* Below left: *John Young takes time to remove a few whiskers.* Below right: *Bob Crippin floats in the cabin in a demonstration of weightlessness. The wire trailing from his head is part of a communications system.*

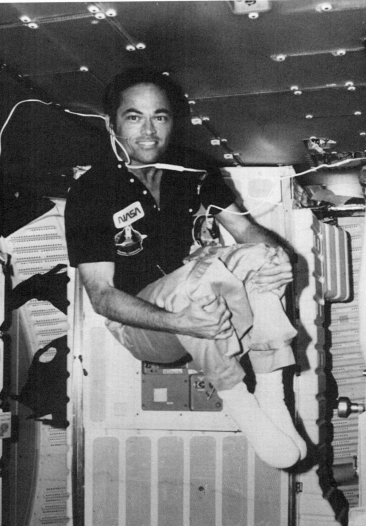

Top: Columbia *touches down on Runway 23 at the Dryden
Flight Research Facility to complete the space portion of STS-1.*
Bottom left: *ground checkout crews greet the STS-1 pioneers.*
Bottom right: *Joe Engle (right) and Dick Truly (left) prepare
to enter* Columbia *and join in the countdown for STS-2.*

problems, virtually all test objectives of the entire program were met. From then on, the shuttle would begin fulfilling its goal as an operational spaceship.

* * * * *

By the end of its fourth flight, the launch profile of the shuttle had become a familiar pattern. On the launch pad, the full stack of the orbiter, external tank, and solid rocket boosters would stand 184.2 feet (56.14 m) tall. Just four seconds before liftoff, the three main engines of the orbiter would ignite. Because the engines normally suck thousands of gallons of propellants from the external tank every minute, they need those four seconds to rev up to full thrust. At the precise moment, the two solid rocket boosters would kick in and the vehicle would be airborne. At first, the climb would be slow but then it would pick up speed. Moments after clearing the launch tower, the nozzles of the engines would begin a slight tilting motion that would rotate the vehicle around so that the back of the orbiter would be facing the direction of the intended orbit.

For the first thunderous minute, the solid rocket engines would fire at full power, but then a trick involving a special shaping of the propellant inside its case would cause a slight reduction of power. It is at this same time that the entire vehicle would pass through the sound barrier, and the lower thrust would ease vibrations. Thrust would then increase until the two boosters would run out of propellants. Approximately 130 seconds after liftoff and at an altitude of 28 miles (45 km), they would be exhausted and separated from the external tank. While the orbiter would continue upward just on the thrust of its three main engines, the boosters would fall back to the ocean. Eventually, large parachutes would slow their fall to make a safe splashdown. Each would partially fill with water and float like a pop bottle until recovery ships could tow it back to shore for reuse on future missions.

The main engines of the orbiter would continue to burn for an additional six and one-half minutes until the propellants in the external tank became exhausted. Then it, too, would separate, but because it was now approximately 70 miles (113 km) above Earth, it would have to reenter the atmosphere. The large silolike tank, unable to handle the stress, would break up as it slammed into the atmosphere. Remaining fragments would splash down in remote ocean areas.

The final thrust for orbit would come from two smaller orbital maneuvering system (OMS) engines mounted in pods that flanked either side of the vertical tail. Each pod would contain enough hydrogen and oxygen propellants for placing the orbiter into orbit, making later orbital adjustments, and finally for braking rocket thrust for return to Earth. The three main engines, once out of propellants, would not be used again until the next launch.

While in orbit, changes in the direction, or attitude, in which the orbiter pointed would be accomplished by forty-two small reaction-control rockets

[41]

Above left: *the space shuttle Atlantis is prepared for its first flight.* Above right: *the glow of the three main orbiter engines' exhaust is overpowered by the brilliant flames coming from the SRB.* Right: *this is an artist's conception of the separation of the SRBs approximately two minutes after launch.*

Left: *the UTC Liberty has docked with a recovered SRB.* Below left: *an artist depicts the separation of the external tank from the orbiter.* Below right: *the tail of the orbiter glows from the exhaust of the orbital maneuvering system engines as they fire.*

strategically placed on the nose and on projections coming off the rear OMS pods. Small thrusts are all that are needed to tilt, roll, and yaw the orbiter.

Following the mission, in which satellites were deployed or retrieved, experiments were conducted, or scientific observations were made, the orbiter would be turned so that it would be traveling tail first. At the precise moment, the OMS engines would fire, diminishing the orbiter's speed just enough to begin its fall back to Earth. The firing would take place halfway around the world from its intended landing strip.

Dropping down from an orbital altitude of perhaps 150 miles (240 km), the orbiter would begin to feel the atmosphere at half that height. With its nose pitched high, friction with the air would heat portions of its underside to over 2,300° F (1,260° C). Sometime following atmospheric contact, the air density would increase sufficiently to permit the wings to take control and produce a thirty-minute-long glide path leading to an airplane landing on the runway. During this time, the airspeed of the orbiter would diminish from around twenty-five times the speed of sound in space to approximately 215 miles per hour (346 kmph) at runway touchdown.

The early missions of the shuttle landed in the California desert to provide a huge landing target to shoot at. The orbiter was then hoisted atop a 747 carrier aircraft for a two-day flight back to the Florida launch site, unlike several later missions that landed instead in Florida.

The actual completion of the mission would take place back in the orbital processing facility at the Kennedy Space Center, where payload bay materials would be removed. From that point on, the vehicle would be made ready for its next flight. Repairs and replacements of parts would be made on the orbiter and its next payload would be inserted. While the orbiter was being checked out, the solid rocket boosters would be erected on the mobile launch pad inside the vehicle assembly building. The external tank would be mounted and attached, and finally, the orbiter would be brought in and hoisted into position. When ready, the full stack vehicle would be moved out to the launch pad for final checkout and loading of the external tank propellants. Several hours before liftoff, the crew would enter and join in on the countdown.

Above: *the 50-foot (15-m) -long Remote Manipulator System arm bends at the elbow during a test of its functions.* Below: *This artist's drawing shows the heating taking place during atmospheric reentry.*

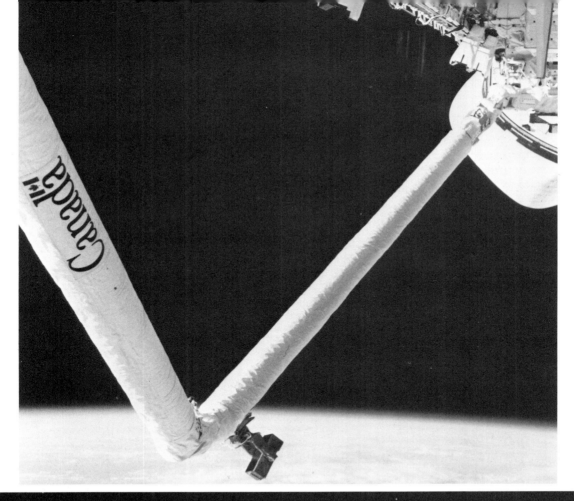

Right: *this is the view out the window of the runway during mission STS-6.* **Below left:** *sections of the SRBs are stacked and joined in the vehicle assembly building.* **Below right:** *two completed SRBs await the joining of the external tank.*

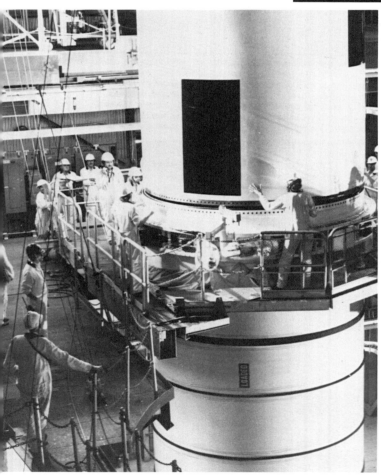

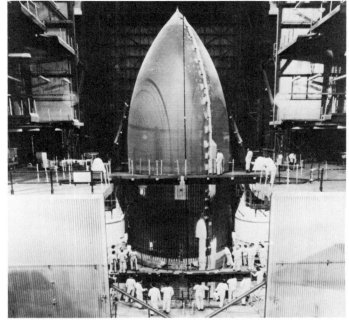

Above left: *the SRBs and external tank are now joined.* **Above right:** *the orbiter is moved to the vehicle assembly building and hoisted for mating with the external tank.* **Left:** *vehicle assembly is completed and the mobile launch pad takes the shuttle to the launch site.*

5

ON BOARD
THE ORBITER

The space shuttle orbiter is an exceptionally versatile spacecraft. It is designed to boost payloads weighing up to 65,000 pounds (29,500 kg) into orbit, deploy satellites, repair and retrieve satellites, and take up parts of giant satellites and space stations for assembly in space. But that is only half of the story. The orbiter crew cabin offers room for a variety of scientific and technological experiments.

The cabin is divided up into two main decks. The upper is known as the flight deck, and it resembles the cockpit of a commercial jetliner. But there are some important differences, including extra computers, special instruments for navigation through space, and joystick controllers for piloting the orbiter instead of the more traditional yoke (steering wheel) used for commercial jets. During liftoff and landing, the pilot sits on the right and the commander on the left. Up to two mission specialists ride in seats just behind the command crew. If other astronauts are on board, they sit in temporary seats on the lower middeck that are folded and stored away to make extra space until it is time for reentry. Up to three mission specialists can sit there. On occasion, a special type of astronaut called a payload specialist may sit there as well. Payload specialists are not career astronauts; they are trained to do jobs specifically related to a particular mission. Payload specialists are usually employed by a company that has contracted with NASA to carry their payload into orbit and want their person to run any tests or experiments related to it.

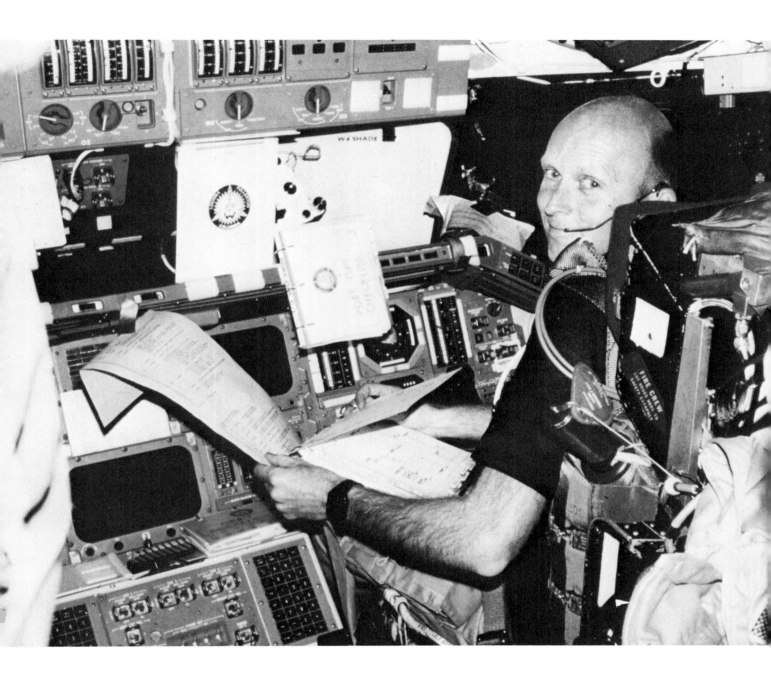

Shuttle pilot Gordon Fullerton reviews teleprinter data from his seat on the flight deck.

Right: *Shannon Lucid monitors payload bay activities from the aft portion of the flight deck. The various controls operate the payload and the Remote Manipulator System arm. Below: the Canadian-built Remote Manipulator System arm is extended in this picture taken from a SPAS-1 satellite that was deployed by the astronauts and retrieved later.*

The rear, or aft, portion of the flight deck is dedicated to the payload bay. Mission specialists stand at control panels facing aft. Two windows look into the bay. From the controls, the astronauts can deploy satellites. First, the satellite is spun on a turntable to give it stability, like a spinning football; then it is ejected. Later, with the orbiter several miles away, a booster rocket on the satellite fires to give it the push needed to send it into proper orbit. In this kind of task, the orbiter serves as a space delivery truck.

The aft controls also work the remote manipulator system arm. The arm, with its six motor-driven joints, can pluck out large payloads from the bay to release them or to grasp free-floating payloads and bring them inside.

The middeck serves as the crew living quarters as well as experiment stations. Along the side wall is the galley, where meals are prepared. Prepackaged foods are prepared here. Some foods are freeze-dried or in powder form. They are held in small plastic boxes that have soft plastic lids. A needle injector device in the galley squirts water into the package, rehydrating the contents. The water can be hot or cold, as needed. Foods that need cooking are placed in an oven. Some of those foods, such as meats, are kept in foil pouches. When the meals are ready, each container is inserted into an aluminum tray and given to the crew members.

Mealtime on the orbiter is invariably a time for play. In the weightless condition of space, the temptation of allowing foods to drift around and float across the cabin is too great for even the most reserved astronauts to resist.

Near the galley, against the back wall, is the lavatory. It is a small, telephone-booth-size cubicle that has a curtain for privacy. A contoured toilet seat with handles and a seat belt rests on top of a platform. Solid wastes are drawn into a bin underneath the platform where a spinning drum, like a garbage disposal, breaks up the waste and compresses it against the inner walls. When the system doesn't work, a "backup" system incorporating plastic bags is employed. Liquid wastes are collected through a funnel and tube arrangement and are directed to a storage tank. After the unit has been used, the solid waste storage tank is opened to outer space so that the vacuum can remove moisture and subsequent odors.

The entire front bulkhead of the middeck is partitioned off with storage lockers. Inside are kept food supplies, experiment apparatus and supplies, personal gear, and sleeping restraints. The restraints are simply sleeping bags with straps for attaching to any convenient surface to prevent drifting about while trying to get a good night's sleep.

The central feature of the aft wall is the airlock compartment. Depending upon the needs of the mission, the compartment may be moved inside the middeck or attached to the outside in the payload bay. On some missions, the airlock is used as the entrance into a special cylindrical science laboratory

Above left: *food packets are heated in preparation for mealtime. Above right: mealtime can be a time for fun as well as for nourishment. Joe Allen enjoys watching a free-floating glob of orange juice.*

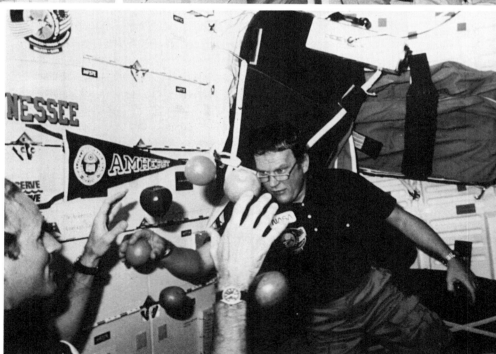

"Here, catch!"

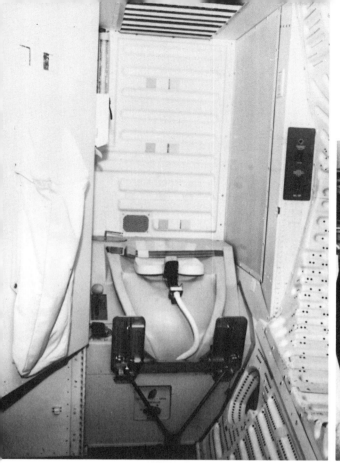

Above left: *the orbiter waste-management compartment (toilet).*
Above right: *Guion Bluford (the first black person in space) works out on a treadmill to retain muscle tone in the weightlessness of Earth orbit.*

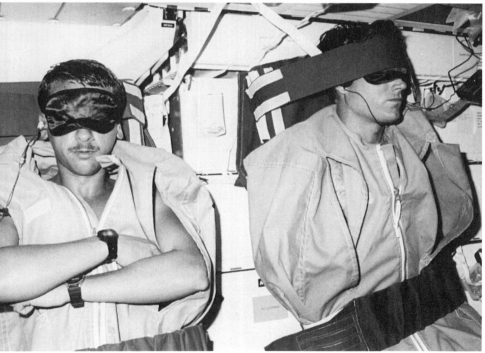

When bedtime comes, crew members slip into sleeping restraints that are attached to the wall.

carried in the bay called *Spacelab*. On other missions, the airlock is the primary staging area for spacewalking. Two crew members don their space suits here and when ready, open the door to the outside. They pull themselves out into the payload bay and attach safety tethers to various rings and wires so that they can move about in safety. When it is necessary to move away from the orbiter to capture a satellite, a spacewalker can back into a cradle that holds a rocket propulsion device called the *manned maneuvering unit* (MMU). The MMU permits total freedom from the orbiter, and the spacewalker becomes temporarily an independent spaceship.

For all its high-tech systems, the space shuttle is really a space truck. Its 60-foot-long (18-m) payload bay is large enough to hold one and one-half school buses. Payloads are what the shuttle is all about.

The shuttle was designed for multiple payload launchings. So far, up to two communications satellites have been carried in the payload bay at one time. On one mission, two satellites were not only deployed but two more previously launched satellites were retrieved. The boosters on the two retrieved satellites were faulty and had failed to transfer them to high orbit. The retrieval operation required two astronauts to suit up and wrestle the satellites into the bay. First they had to stabilize them; they accomplished this by flying the manned maneuvering unit and inserting a special capture device called a "stinger" into the nozzle of the spent rocket booster. Later, the satellites were brought into the bay with the mechanical arm and stowed in the same brackets used to hold the two satellites just released.

On other spacewalking missions, astronauts have practiced assembling large structures to evaluate assembly techniques for bringing up future large satellites and segments of a space station too large to be carried up on just one flight. As the segments are brought up, they will be joined together. This launch technology, yet to be tried with an actual payload by shuttle crews, opens many future opportunities for building large space structures.

Above left: *Payload Specialist Charles Walker checks out a protein crystal growth experiment. Walker is employed by McDonnell-Douglas, an industrial aerospace firm.* **Above right:** *Jerry Ross leaves the airlock for a spacewalk in the payload bay.* **Below:** *STS-5 crew members use a sign to brag about deploying two satellites.*

The ANIK C-3 communications satellite is spun to make it stable and then ejected from its cradle on the STS-5 mission.

Above: *Bruce McCandless becomes the first free-flying astronaut as he tests the new manned maneuvering unit (MMU) on flight 41-B. Facing page: techniques for assembling future large space structures are experimented with during spacewalks on flight 61-B.*

Many payloads of the shuttle have been designed to be carried into space and returned at the completion of the mission. Often, these payloads were designed for study of the Earth from space. At orbital altitudes, the shuttle can view large portions of the Earth at a time, permitting correlation of many observations at once. Thunderstorms can be studied from above. Radar maps showing subsurface details can detect ancient buried river channels and archaeological sites. Geological structures of the Earth can be identified, helping to predict earthquake hazard areas and possible new mineral resource sites.

Because of the large payload bay, many payloads simply do not fill its capacity. NASA foresaw many open spaces on its planned missions and began offering a special payload class to the public called the "Getaway Special." Essentially, the payload is a small canister about the size of a trash can that can be mounted in the bay whenever there is room. Anyone with an idea for a scientific or technological experiment can rent one of these containers and have their experiment flown in space. Dozens of experiments have already been flown and hundreds more are waiting for launch.

The most elaborate payload flown so far by the shuttle is Spacelab. Spacelab has many different configurations, but, essentially, it is a cylindrical laboratory about 23 feet (7 m) long that is mounted partway back in the bay. A tunnel connects the airlock of the middeck to the lab entrance. Inside, the lab is well equipped to run many experiments simultaneously. There is also a small airlock for apparatus that needs to be exposed to space and for specialized cameras aimed outward. There are numerous experiment racks that hold everything from chemical and metallurgical experiments to cages for rats and monkeys.

Each time Spacelab flies it is configured to the specific needs of the experiments aboard. Between missions, the lab is removed from the bay and old apparatus is replaced with new apparatus.

Spacelab also has a secondary facility called the *pallet*, a U-shaped rack that serves as a back porch to Spacelab on some missions. Located outside, the pallet provides a firm mounting base for experiments that are either too large to be carried inside the laboratory or that need continuous exposure to outer space. When Spacelab is not flying, science experiments are carried out on the middeck.

Left: Dale Gardner approaches an errant satellite with his MMU. A capture device, called the "stinger," will attach itself to the satellite to slow its spin; the satellite can then be brought back on board the orbiter. Below: following capture, the satellite is "wrestled" into the payload bay.

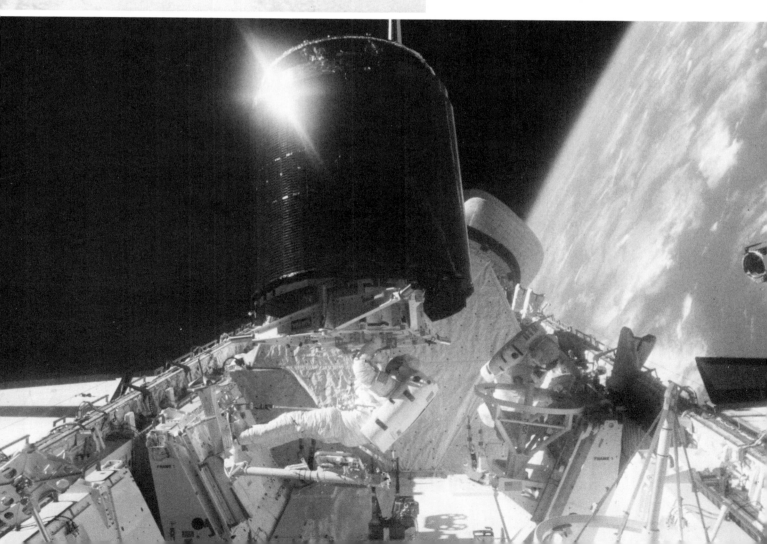

Above left: *folded rock in mountainous regions of Mexico clearly show their structure to the orbiting shuttle crew.* Above right: *thunderstorms are seen from above on mission STS-6.*

Spacelab 1 is visible in the payload bay during the STS-9 mission. The laboratory is connected to the orbiter middeck by a tunnel. The outside of the laboratory is covered with insulating fabric.

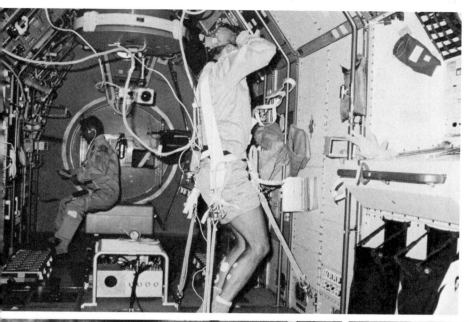

Spacelab provides extra room on the orbiter for a wide variety of experiments.

Below left: *William Thornton checks to see how a monkey in a cage aboard Spacelab is doing. Below right: Jack Lousma checks out the bugs on STS-3. The plastic box encloses flying insects that were added to the mission's experiment roster by high school student Todd Nelson.*

FLIGHT OF THE *CHALLENGER*

The shuttle orbiter *Challenger* was the second orbiter to fly. It became the shuttle fleet's workhorse vehicle while *Columbia* was being refurbished in the assembly plant and while the orbiters *Discovery* and *Atlantis* were being finished. By January 1986, all four orbiters had achieved flight status, but *Challenger* held the record—nine successful flights.

Challenger had been used to launch and repair satellites, carry Spacelab, conduct experiments, and study the Earth's surface. Its January 28, 1986, flight was supposed to be an interesting departure from previous space missions. Along with six regular crew members was schoolteacher Christa McAuliffe, who had won a national competition for the honor of being the first teacher to conduct class from outer space.

Several delays had pushed the launch attempt back to the twenty-eighth. The night before, freezing weather had dropped the vehicle's temperature to dangerous levels as icicles formed on launch-pad structures. Still it was thought that the vehicle was safe to fly. It was a disastrous decision. Seventy-three seconds after liftoff, the external tank exploded in a huge fireball, destroying *Challenger* and killing its crew of seven.

The nation and the world were stunned. The loss of a shuttle was always a possibility, but the string of twenty-four straight successful launches had convinced nearly everyone that shuttle flights were routine.

The crew of mission 51-L leave the operations and checkout building to board a van that will take them to the launch pad. They are, front to back: Commander Francis Scobee, Mission Specialists Judith Resnik and Ron McNair, Pilot Michael Smith, Teacher-Observer Christa McAuliffe, Mission Specialist Ellison Onizuka, and Payload Specialist Gregory Jarvis.

Left: *the Challenger lifts off at 11:38 a.m. EST carrying its crew of seven*

Right: *at 66.625 seconds into launch, no one is yet aware of the disaster about to take place.*

Three seconds after the explosion, billowing white clouds nearly obscure debris from the shattered vehicle.

Months of vehicle-fragment recovery operations, reconstructions, and investigations pinpointed the cause. Replays of launch films picked up a puff of smoke coming from one of the lower joints of the right solid rocket booster. Flames were seen between the external tank and orbiter as the vehicle climbed skyward.

Ironically, the shuttle system technology best understood and seemingly the most reliable ultimately caused the disaster. Frigid prelaunch temperatures led to the failure of rubber seals of one of the right booster's joints. A blowtorch-like flame shot out sideways from the joint and licked the lower external tank wall where the liquid hydrogen was kept. While burning a hole through the insulation and tank wall, the flames also severed the lower supports holding the booster to the tank. The booster was able to pivot, and its upper end forced an opening in the upper oxygen tank, permitting the oxygen to stream out to mix with the hydrogen and detonate.

The crew cabin with the seven on board was blown away from the vehicle. The explosion force and the loss of cabin pressure is believed to have either killed crew members immediately or caused them to lose consciousness as the cabin lost pressure and fell 10 miles (16 km), smashing into the ocean below. No one survived.

GROUNDED

The American manned space program ground to a halt. None of the remaining three shuttles will fly again until teams of scientists and engineers from NASA and industry develop new technologies and procedures to prevent a similar loss of shuttles in the future.

Many areas of vehicle redesign are being considered. Most important is a redesign of the booster joints. Normally, the solid rocket boosters are assembled from four main segments. They are erected on the launchpad with fuel already loaded in each segment. The lower rim of each joint has a groove for receiving a tongue from the upper rim. Rubber O-ring seals press against the two metals to keep in the pressure of the burning rocket gases. A special putty is also placed at various points to assist in sealing the joint.

The fixed booster joint is likely to have an extra rim of metal on the inside and a third O-ring seal to strengthen the joint. Existing O-ring rubber will be replaced with a material more resistant to lower temperatures.

Although it is not likely that the crew of the *Challenger* could have survived the explosion even if their vehicle had been equipped with an escape system, other potential launch problems might be survivable with some such system. One hazardous period of flight takes place following reentry when the orbiter becomes an unpowered glider airplane. Any malfunction of control surfaces

Right: replays of videotapes of the launch reveal a puff of black smoke appearing near the base of the external tank, near the right SRB. Far right: another clue to the mishap is an unusual plume of flame in the area of the right SRB as the vehicle climbs skyward.

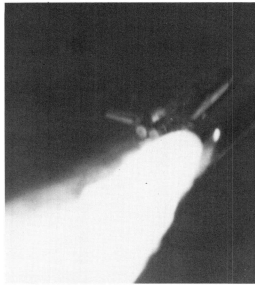

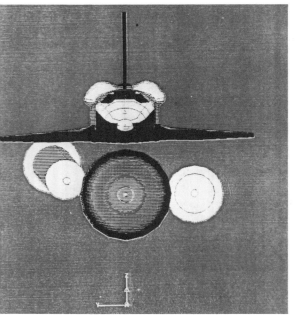

Left: a computer simulation shows a loose right SRB crashing into the side wall of the liquid oxygen portion of the external tank. Right: recovered debris from the Challenger is lowered to the shore from a search vessel.

on the wings or falling short of the landing runway could quickly lead to disaster. An escape system for use during this phase of flight is planned. It is a cradle-like device that will be mounted just inside the orbiter's side entryway hatch. In an emergency, the hatch will be blown away by explosive charges and crew members, one at a time, will climb into position and be dragged out of the orbiter by high-speed rockets. When clear of the vehicle, a parachute will open to bring each crew member safely down. Such a system could also be used in an aborted launch attempt when it is not possible to reach orbit and the orbiter is unable to glide all the way to an emergency landing site. The system will also have an inflatable slide, like commercial airplanes do, for emergency exit of an orbiter after it has landed.

Other areas of changes to the space shuttle program will include improved landing systems, parachute-ejection system, improved landing gear brakes, and better local weather forecasting of the landing site. After shuttle flights resume, the first landings will again take place on the desert runways of the Dryden Flight Research Facility in California. The extremely long runways there provide an additional safety factor.

NASA is also reexamining its schedule of launches to make sure that it doesn't try to cram in too many flights in too short a time. It has canceled plans for a modified Centaur booster stage to be carried in the payload bay. The Centaur is a high-energy liquid hydrogen and oxygen rocket ideal for launching heavy interplanetary probes toward Jupiter and beyond. In light of the loss of the *Challenger*, the rocket was judged to be too hazardous to be carried in the payload bay. NASA has also cut back on the number of communications satellites it will launch with the shuttle and will encourage customers to use expendable rockets instead. Stepped-up quality control and improved communications among launch managers is also planned. NASA further hopes to move veteran astronauts into greater management functions to take advantage of their "on the job" experience.

NEW ORBITER

NASA plans to erect a permanent space station in orbit by the mid-1990s. Essential to those plans is the heavy payload capacity of shuttle orbiters. With three orbiters, the job would take too long. For this reason as well as for the mounting backlog of payloads grounded with the shuttles, a replacement fourth orbiter has now been started. NASA administrators are even pressing for a fifth orbiter to be built, perhaps with private financing.

The resumption of shuttle flights depends upon many factors. It is possible they will be up and flying by early 1988, but delays could push flight schedules back to 1999. In the meantime, many communications, weather, and military

[67]

satellite payloads need to be launched. When the space shuttle was first proposed, it was supposed to be a replacement for nearly all expendable launch vehicles. The *Challenger* tragedy has led to a rethinking of that idea. Expendable launch vehicles can be an economical and safer alternative to the shuttle for payload launches that do not require astronaut assistance. As the shuttle is modified and made ready, America's space program will return to the concept of a "mixed fleet" of manned and unmanned space vehicles.

7

NEW WINGED SPACESHIPS

Years ago, as the United States prepared for its first space shuttle launch, the rest of the world's space community watched with great interest. Would the reusable spaceship work? The idea proved sound, and even with the *Challenger* tragedy, worldwide enthusiasm for winged spaceships has not dampened. Today, other spacefaring nations of the world are at work designing or building at least five different shuttle vehicles taking advantage of America's experience. In fact, one of the new winged spaceship designs is practically a clone of the American shuttle.

HERMES, THE WINGED SPACEPLANE

Since 1979, the European Space Agency has been a competitor with the United States in the satellite launch business. It has built a family of rockets called "Ariane." The family has grown to four rockets, and a fifth member, the *Ariane 5*, is expected to join sometime in the mid-1990s. *Ariane 5* will be a versatile rocket that can serve both as an unmanned expendable launch vehicle and as a manned launcher boosting a returnable shuttle vehicle.

The *Ariane 5*, as an unmanned booster, will stand approximately 170 feet (52 m) tall and have a payload lift capacity to a low orbit of 33,000 pounds (15,000 kg). It will have a central liquid hydrogen/oxygen rocket flanked with two solid rocket boosters in an arrangement similar to the space shuttle's boost-

[69]

ers and external tank. As a manned booster, the payload section above the central rocket will be replaced with a delta-winged manned spaceship—*Hermes*.

Hermes is planned to be much smaller than the American shuttle orbiter. ESA believes that using the same launcher for manned and unmanned missions will accomplish virtually the same jobs as the shuttle can—with the exception of bringing back heavy payloads to Earth—at a lower cost and higher degree of safety for the crew.

In one *Hermes* design under consideration, the wingtips of the delta-winged spacecraft will be upturned to form two vertical tails. Other versions have up to three vertical tails. Otherwise, the vehicle will look like a small space shuttle. The crew of four to six will sit forward in the nose much like in a commercial jetliner. The back will open to reveal a cylindrical cargo bay 9 feet (3 m) in diameter and 16 feet (5 m) long. It will be able to carry approximately 10,000 pounds (4,500 kg) of payload. Outwardly, *Hermes* will be 52 feet (16 m) long, and its wingspan will stretch 33 feet (10 m).

During the launch phase, *Hermes* will sit directly on top of the central booster. Although the overall vehicle shape is somewhat different, its flight profile is very similar to the flight plans of Werner von Braun's 1950s reusable launcher proposal. Midway into the launch, *Hermes* will separate from the booster and continue up into space on the power of two engines located in its tail. Originally, *Hermes* had only one engine, but the *Challenger* explosion motivated designers to increase *Hermes'* safety factor. If mission abort becomes necessary, four powerful ejection motors will separate *Hermes* from the booster; then the two onboard engines will pull it away and give it maneuvering power to return to the landing site. Another safety modification being considered is an ejectable crew cabin. On a successful flight, the engines will boost *Hermes* into orbit while smaller engines do the orbital maneuvering. Following a deorbit burn, at the end of the mission, *Hermes* will reenter the atmosphere like the space shuttle and return to a runway landing near its launch site. The launch site is located close to the Earth's equator in French Guiana in South America, where the *Ariane*s are presently being launched.

Typical *Hermes* missions will include flying up to service unmanned orbital space platforms and carrying crew and supplies to space stations. ESA expects

The **Hermes** *will be much smaller than the U.S. space shuttle and will have a cargo bay that is about 9 feet (2.7 m) in diameter.*

[70]

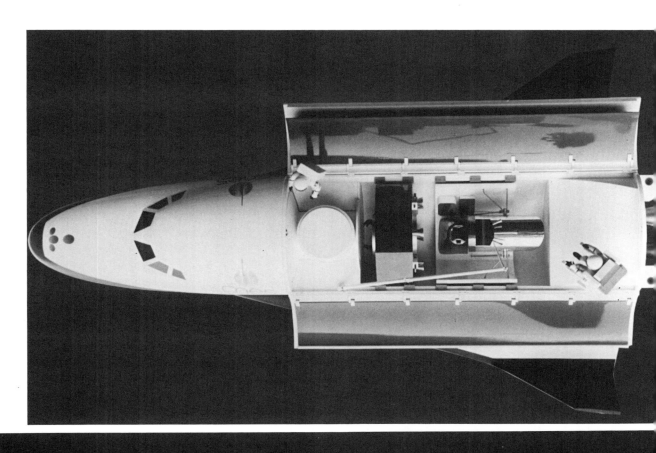

to use *Hermes* four to six times a year after the proposed permanent American space station becomes operational in the mid-1990s. With *Hermes*, ESA will become a full partner with the United States in space exploration.

SOVIET SHUTTLES

The Soviet Union is the most experienced and committed of all the spacefaring nations. In a typical year it will launch nearly a hundred satellites and manned missions. Since Yuri Gagarin's historic flight in 1961, Soviet cosmonauts have accumulated the equivalent of twelve years of manned spaceflight experience. This is more than twice the total flight experience of the U.S. manned program.

In spite of their great number of space flights, the Soviet space program is shrouded in secrecy. The Soviets usually acknowledge a spaceflight only after it has been successfully launched, and even then details are sketchy. Most information about current and future Soviet space activities comes from a variety of sources, including reconnaissance satellite photographs and intelligence reports. Diverse bits of information are studied until trends become apparent. From such bits, Western space experts believe the Soviet Union is embarked on building at least one and possibly two shuttle vehicles.

One Soviet shuttle falls into the same class as the American space shuttle and the other is comparable to ESA's *Hermes*. The large Soviet shuttle is so similar to the American vehicle that the two would be nearly indistinguishable at a distance. The primary difference between the two orbiters is located in the tail region. The Soviet orbiter has its main engines mounted on the base of the external fuel tank and not on its tail, where the American orbiter's main engines are located. This means that the engines will be discarded along with the external tank, but it does provide Soviet designers with extra space to mount foldaway jet engines that will yield increased maneuverability on landing approach. Presumably, the jet engines will provide a safety margin in case unexpected headwinds pound the orbiter as it approaches the runway. If such an event took place with the unpowered approach of an American shuttle, the loss of ground speed could result in a crash landing.

Instead of the main engines, two small orbital maneuvering system engines are mounted on the tail of the orbiter. These serve the same function as the OMS engines of the American counterpart. No details of the vehicle's interior are available yet, though the cargo bay is thought to be able to carry up to 66,000 pounds (30,000 kg) of payload.

During launch, the large Soviet shuttle will be mounted to the side of a large external tank. Four strap-on liquid fuel boosters will be mounted to the tank as well. The liquid boosters, designated SL-X-16, are the Soviets' first use

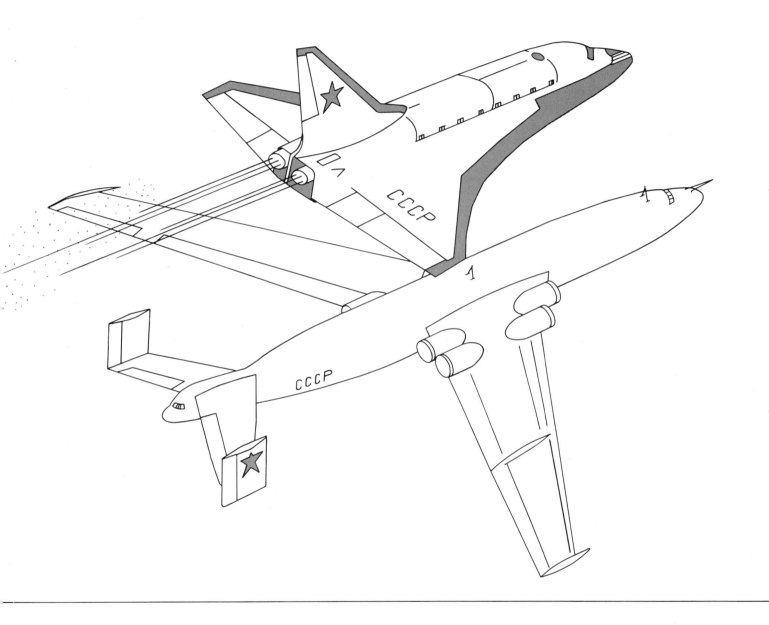

The Soviet space shuttle orbiter rises off its Bison Myasishchev Mya-4 bomber aircraft in this drawing showing an approach and landing test.

of liquid hydrogen/liquid oxygen rocket engines and will generate a total of 5.2 million pounds (23.3 million newtons) of thrust. Including the main engines on the external tank, liftoff thrust will total 6.6 million pounds (29.6 million newtons). The combined booster, external tank, and orbiter weight is approximately 4.4 million pounds (2 million kg).

The launch site will be the Baikonur Cosmodrome in Siberia, a launch facility the size of nine Kennedy Space Centers combined. A large shuttle runway, easily seen from satellite photographs, has been built near the launch pad.

In planning their large shuttle, the Soviets have considered unmanned launch needs as well. A 120-foot-long (37-m) cargo carrier can be launched with the external tank and boosters instead of the orbiter, for a total lift capacity into orbit of 220,000 pounds (100,000 kg). This would enable the Soviets to boost large space station components similar in size to the American *Skylab*.

Multiple use has also been planned for the SL-X-16 boosters. They can be used for medium-weight unmanned payloads or, as some Western space experts believe, for a small spaceplane. The small spaceplane has been tested in suborbital flights and recovered by parachute twice from the Indian Ocean and twice from the Black Sea. The use of the spaceplane is debatable. Some consider its function to be a quick-response military vehicle capable of getting crews up into space in a relatively short time. It has also been suggested that the spaceplane is really a bomb-delivery system that could "drop in" on the U.S. fleet during a war.

At the time of this writing, neither Soviet shuttle appears to have been tested in space with human crews. The Soviets have begun testing their large shuttle in a program similar to the tests in which the American space shuttle was carried on the back of a 747 carrier aircraft and dropped for practice landings. Western experts believe the first space flights may be imminent.

JAPANESE SHUTTLE

The island country of Japan is rapidly becoming a world space power. The Japanese have moved into the satellite launch business and have constructed extensive rocket launch and research facilities. They have also entered the planetary exploration field by sending out spacecraft to study Halley's Comet during its most recent approach, in 1986. Japan, like other emerging space-power nations, is also looking toward manned space flight. It has begun tests on a shuttlelike vehicle of its own.

Japan's National Aerospace Laboratory has begun preliminary research to determine if a manned shuttle is a technically and economically feasible project for its country to pursue. Currently, the proposed Japanese shuttle is viewed as an incremental program, beginning first with an ESA *Hermes*-style vehicle by 1995 and growing into a vehicle that could possibly take off from an airport runway for a direct flight into space by the year 2010.

Japanese researchers have been testing a variety of shuttle designs, including some that look like small versions of the American space shuttle and others that look like the *Hermes*. Wind-tunnel tests have been conducted with vehicles featuring a single vertical stabilizer tail, twin tails, and no tails but with upturned wingtips. All models so far, no bigger than 1 foot (0.3 m) in size, are based on a delta-shaped wing design with the crew sitting in the nose and a payload bay built into the vehicle's back. Larger models have also been carried up thousands of feet above the Pacific Ocean and dropped to test their handling characteristics.

The initial Japanese shuttle would be mounted to the nose of a Japanese H-1 rocket launcher for its boost into space. Later, a larger shuttle vehicle will be made ready for launch with an H-2 rocket that will be upgraded in thrust by the addition of at least four strap-on solid rocket boosters. This second-generation shuttle would have air intakes so that its engines could take advantage of atmospheric oxygen to reduce the amount of liquid oxygen carried. Such a vehicle would be a logical intermediate step to an aerospace plane of the future able to operate from airport runways.

SPACE TRANSPORTATION FOR THE TWENTY-FIRST CENTURY

By the early twenty-first century, the American space shuttle and possibly space shuttles of other nations will be obsolete. The American shuttle, at its outset, was theoretically supposed to be far less expensive, more versatile, and easier to launch than expendable heavy-lift launch vehicles. It has proved its versatility, but cost savings were not as great as hoped and turnaround time to send it back into space was far greater than planned. The quick and relatively easy space-launch system proposed by Werner von Braun in the early 1950s still remains elusive.

In the twenty-first century, von Braun's goal could be achieved by a new hybrid airplane/space vehicle. The United States, United Kingdom, and West Germany are each interested in such a vehicle. In the United States the vehicle envisioned has been called, variously, the hypersonic transport, the transatmospheric vehicle, the "Orient Express," or, officially, the National Aero-Space Plane. The United Kingdom version is called HOTOL, an acronym for "horizontal takeoff and landing." West Germany calls its vehicle the Sanger.

"NASP"

Imagine boarding a dart-shaped airplane in Washington, D.C., at noon and stepping off in Tokyo, Japan, two hours later. Traveling halfway around the world in just two hours is only a commercial application of America's proposed

[76]

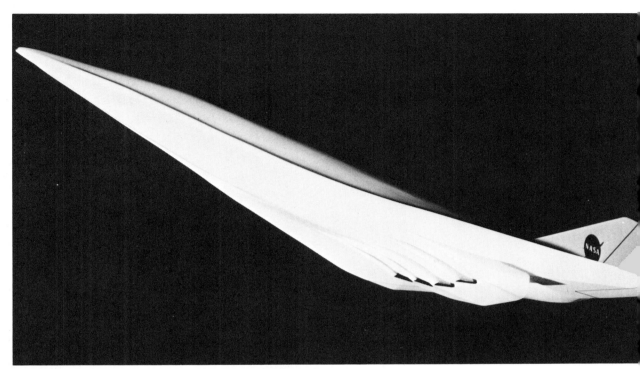

Early concepts (1971) of hypersonic transport aircraft that would carry passengers at a speed of 4,000 miles per hour (6,400 kmph). Studies of these and other designs contributed to the National Aero-Space Plane concept.

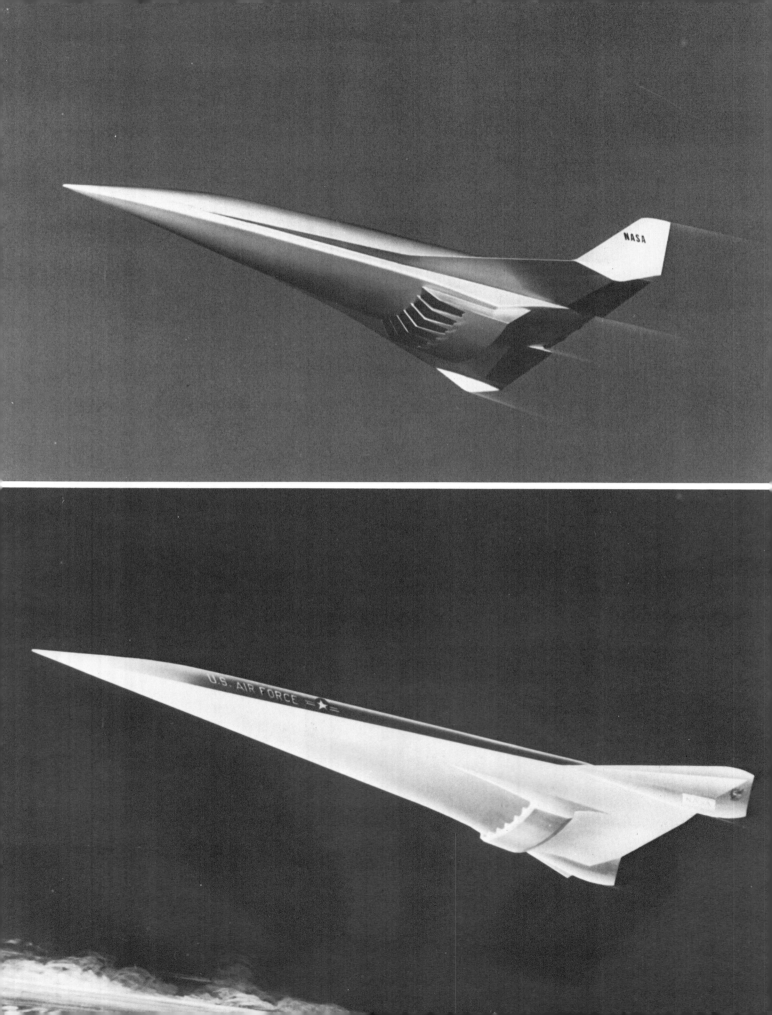

National Aero-Space Plane (NASP). Commercial airlines would operate the NASP on international routes. It would fly at more than twelve times the speed of sound (mach) and climb to altitudes of more than 20 miles (32 km). NASA and air force versions of the NASP would reach orbital speeds of 25 mach and carry satellites and planetary probes, space-station supplies, and military payloads into orbit at costs much lower than the space shuttle could accomplish.

The NASP would be unlike any previous space vehicle because it would launch itself directly into space from an airport runway without dropping off lower stages. To keep costs low, it would use as many as three types of engines to achieve orbit. A turbojet engine similar to that used in today's jetliners would be used for takeoff. Spinning compressor fan blades would suck air in through an inlet and compress it before sending it into the combustion chamber for mixing with liquid hydrogen fuel for ignition. As supersonic speeds are reached, the air entering the inlet will become compressed on its own, and by mach 3 there will no longer be a need for compressor blades. Engines operating at this speed are called *ramjets*. The NASP will probably have some sort of hybrid engine combining both turbo and ramjet features. By the time the NASP reaches mach 6, it will still only be in "first gear." At that point, a more efficient supersonic combustion ramjet (a "scramjet") would take over, accelerating the vehicle into "second gear." The final jump into orbit would be accomplished by "third gear" rocket engines.

Using a multiengine design will enable the NASP to be more efficient than expendable launch vehicles or the space shuttle. It would have to carry oxygen only for its rocket engines—the lower-speed engines would draw oxygen directly from the atmosphere.

As a space vehicle, the NASP would operate in orbit very much like the space shuttle. On the way back down, like the shuttle, it would have to reenter the atmosphere. But, unlike the shuttle, its engines could be started up for a powered return to an airport runway.

Development of the NASP is being shared by NASA and the U.S. Air Force. The prototype vehicle, the X-30, is expected to cost between $2 billion and

Here are two alternate 1985 concepts of an aerospace plane capable of airport runway takeoff and climb to low-Earth orbit. These concepts use both air-breathing and rocket engines during flight.

$3 billion and be ready for test flights by the early to mid-1990s. When the operational vehicle is ready, the NASP should be able to carry payloads into orbit at a cost of about 10 percent of that of the space shuttle—that is, for less than $200 per pound (0.45 kg).

In spite of its great potential, the NASP is a risky venture. It is based on technology that has yet to be developed. Delays in its development could put the American space program on a multiyear hold in the early twenty-first century, after the existing space shuttle fleet is due to retire from service. NASA is concerned about the possible gap between the old shuttles and the beginning of regular service with the NASP and so is considering building an in-between space vehicle that will begin shuttling to and from the planned space station shortly after the year 2000.

The proposed new vehicle is referred to by some as "shuttle 2" because it somewhat resembles the existing space shuttles. However, it would feature major improvements, especially in the area of weight. The present shuttles can lift only about 10 percent of their dry weight (weight without propellants) into space. Through the use of superlight construction materials, shuttle 2 could lift up to 100 percent of its dry weight. Obviously, such a vehicle could achieve major savings over the existing shuttles.

Shuttle 2 is planned as a single-stage rocket that would be launched vertically. (Some versions under consideration feature a retrievable second stage.) Its exact specifications are yet to be determined, but it could be 163 feet (50 m) long and have a payload capacity ranging from 20,000 to 50,000 pounds (9,100 to 22,700 kg). Viewed from above, its wings would be much smaller than the space shuttle's and its wingtips would be turned up to form tails. The central tail of the space shuttle would be absent. Like the space shuttle, the crew cabin would be in front and the engines in the rear. However, up to seven engines would be present. They would burn liquid hydrocarbon (petroleum-based fuel)

Above: *the National Aero-Space Plane approaches a rendezvous with the U.S. manned space station. Other versions of the plane will be used for commercial airline service.* **Below:** *a shuttle 2 orbiter approaches a space platform. This version of the shuttle 2 features a two-stage rocket and a vertical launch.*

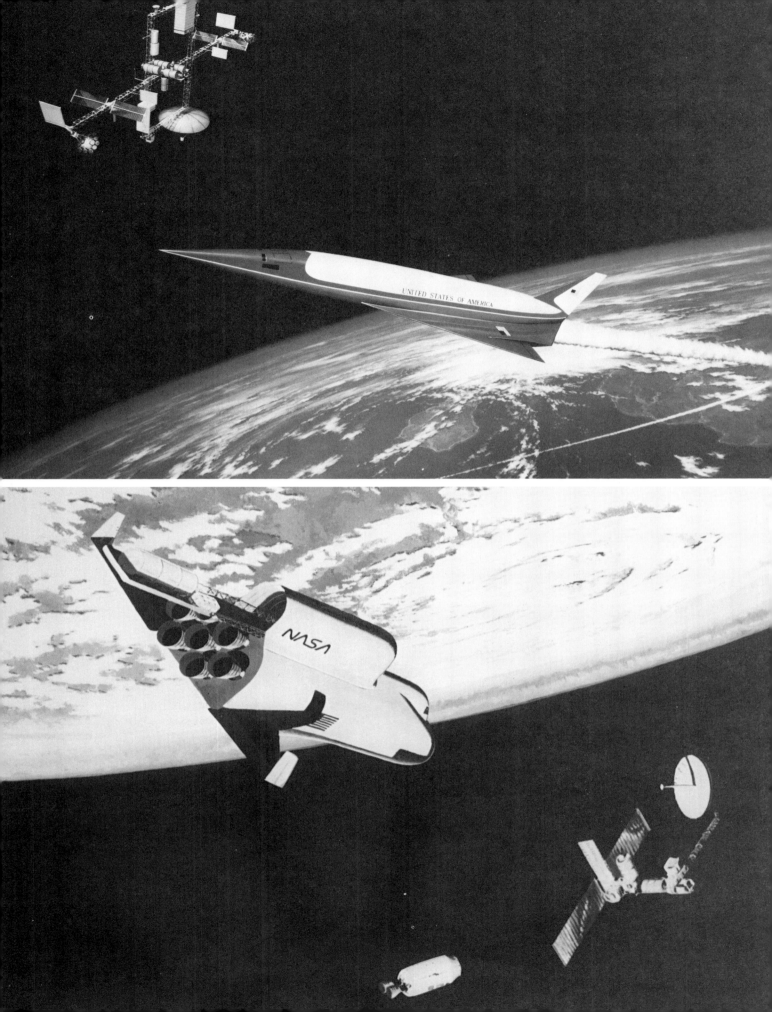

and liquid oxygen. Some versions being considered replace the hydrocarbon with hydrogen and others use both but at different parts of the flight.

Fuel for shuttle 2 would be contained in tanks in its belly. Payload would be carried in a bulging canister on its back. The canister would be detachable, which would make payload processing on the ground much faster than is possible now. Currently, entire shuttle orbiters must be taken into the payload facility for processing. Just the shuttle 2 canisters would be processed while the vehicle was being erected on the launch pad and checked out for flight.

Many questions about the shuttle 2 concept have yet to be answered before NASA can commit itself to building it. If it is approved, the first full-scale tests could be made by the year 2000, and operational service would begin a year or two later.

HOTOL

HOTOL, the British version of the American NASP, is expected to operate in much the same manner. In its early design stage, HOTOL is envisioned to be 250 feet (76 m) long and have a delta-shaped wingspan of 66 feet (20 m). Its payload bay, mounted midship, is about the diameter of the bay of the space shuttle. For commercial transportation service, the bay can be fitted with about sixty seats for people wanting to fly halfway around the world in just one hour. For space use, the bay could hold up to 7 tons of payload.

Like the NASP, HOTOL will take advantage of atmospheric oxygen for the climb into space and carry liquid oxygen for space use. This will lead to major launch-cost-per-pound savings over that of the space shuttle. The nose tank of HOTOL will hold liquid hydrogen and the aft tank (behind the payload section) will hold liquid oxygen.

One interesting feature of the HOTOL takeoff is that the landing gear of the vehicle will be retracted. It will rest, instead, on a wheeled trolley. Thrust from the engines will propel HOTOL along the runway, and the trolley will give it support until it is airborne on its own.

Above: this early model of the HOTOL aerospace plane shows the position of the payload bay near the vertical tails. The nose features three fins for control. Below: a more recent version of HOTOL has a shortened nose, only one fin up front, and no vertical tails in the rear.

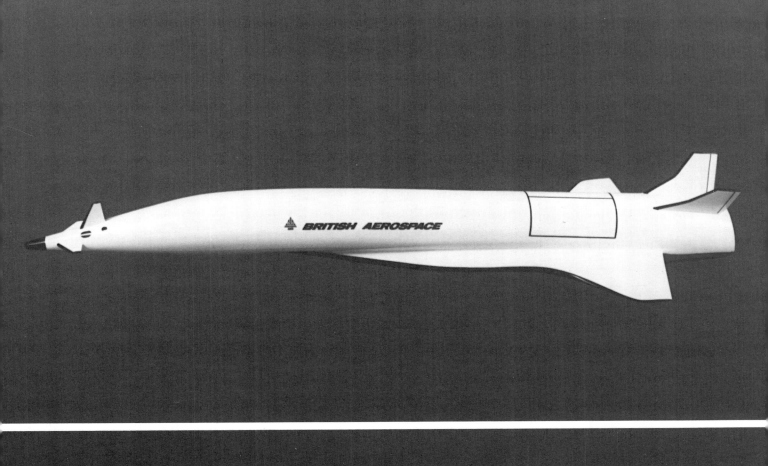

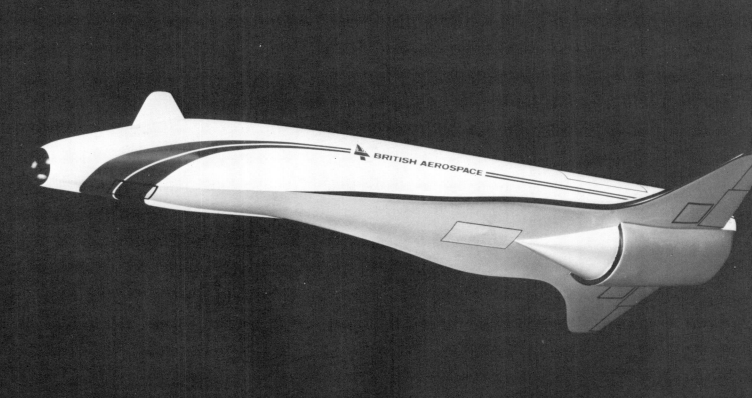

The Sanger, as pictured here, would be able to take off
from any airfield on Earth and carry payloads into space.

Air tests of HOTOL should begin in 1996, and, if successful, it is hoped it will be ready for service early in the twenty-first century, first as an unmanned launch vehicle and later as a manned vehicle. The development cost of HOTOL is steep, more than $6 billion. The United Kingdom hopes to enlist the other members of the European Space Agency to join in its development. If not, they may look to American industry to link up with them.

GERMAN SANGER
SPACE TRANSPORT SYSTEM

One final entry into the aerospace plane competition comes from West Germany. The Germans have proposed a two-stage winged transport that would take off from an airport runway. At takeoff, it would look something like a space shuttle orbiter resting on top of a 747 carrier aircraft. The carrier aircraft would feature air-breathing engines and accelerate the mated vehicles to a velocity of mach 6 at an altitude of 18.6 miles (30 m) before the two vehicles would separate. The piloted carrier aircraft would then fly back to an airport runway while the space vehicle would continue upward to space on the power of its liquid hydrogen/oxygen engine.

The Germans call their winged spaceship the Sanger space transport system, Sanger for short. They envision it as a follow-up to the space shuttle/*Hermes* generation of space launch vehicles.

Sanger's first stage would be a relatively flat delta-winged vehicle with upturned wingtips to act as vertical stabilizers. Its length would be 164 feet (50 m) and wingspan 82 feet (25 m). It would be propelled by turbo-ramjet engines that could operate subsonically and supersonically.

The second stage would be considerably smaller than the first, with a length of 82 feet (25 m) and wingspan of 40 feet (12 m). It would carry its liquid hydrogen in an elongated tank that the crew would literally sit on. The oxygen would be located in a spherical tank to the rear, just in front of the engine.

The Germans would like to have the European Space Agency build the Sanger because they consider it a less risky alternative to the U.K.'s HOTOL. They point out that though theoretically possible, no one has ever built the kind of engines HOTOL would require. Sanger, they believe, could launch payloads into space at a cost of one-fourth that of the space shuttle. At first it could carry a crew of two, ten passengers, and a cargo of up to 4 tons. Later versions could be converted to passenger use for up to 200 passengers for intercontinental flights of 8,000 miles (12,900 km), making it competitive with the American NASP.

[85]

ROCKETING INTO
THE FUTURE

Werner von Braun's dream of human space travel has been realized, but his dream was much more than just the method of getting there. It was the dream of space as the next human frontier where people would work, live, and explore.

In the nearly thirty years since Yuri Gagarin rode into space with humankind's tentative hopes for the future, human space travel has become almost routine. Each of us is touched daily by the benefits of space research through our communications, weather forecasting, medical care, ground and air trans-portation, food we eat, and products we buy.

What will our future in space bring? Certainly more exploration and more of the same benefits as before but on a far grander scale. In near-Earth orbit there will be space stations (two Soviet stations are up there now), giant sat-ellites, manufacturing facilities, and spaceports. These various facilities will be serviced by winged spaceships.

Most likely, only some of the seven or more proposed new winged space-ships and aerospace planes will be built to join or replace the space shuttle. Those that do will open the door to space travel for nonastronauts—average people who will visit other space facilities, perhaps orbiting hotels for people on vacation. Others will visit space only briefly while on their way to destinations halfway around the world.

Economical space transport will change the near-Earth environment of space. Space stations of the future won't have to be cleverly designed compact

Above: future space stations will be made possible by winged spaceships that will carry up the components for orbital assembly. Below: when operational, space stations of the 1990s and beyond will be serviced by winged spaceships bringing up supplies and crew.

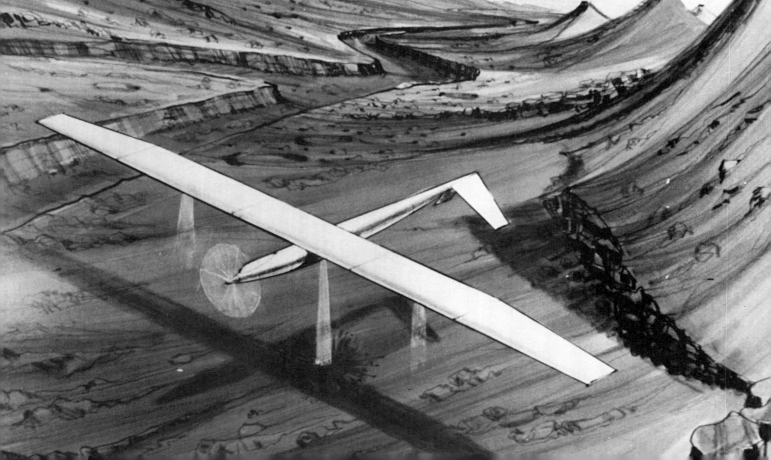

cylinders. They will be large complexes, perhaps the size of small Earth towns. They will be centers for the manufacturing of products better made in the weightless condition of Earth orbit than on the Earth itself. They will be jumping-off points for journeys to the Moon and Mars, where permanently manned scientific laboratories and colonies will be set up.

Spaceships destined for the Moon won't need wings in the vacuum of space, but they will be brought into space for assembly by winged spaceships. Spaceships heading for Mars won't need wings either but will probably rendezvous in Mars orbit with winged ships designed to shuttle down through the thin Martian atmosphere to the Martian surface and go back into orbit again. Beyond Mars, humans will move out to the moons of Jupiter and Saturn and ultimately to the far reaches of the galaxy.

Predictions for our future in space have been made by space experts for decades. It is fascinating to look back to see what was predicted and compare it with what has actually happened. Specific details are usually different, but the overall predictions, like von Braun's of pushing our frontier into space, have come true. The winged spaceship needed for von Braun's wheel-shaped space station has yet to come to pass, but one descendant of his idea has flown in space twenty-four times and others are close on the horizon. Though shapes and timetables have changed, his dream is alive.

Above: *A lunar ferry craft in the twenty-first century prepares to break Earth orbit with supplies for the lunar colony. Components of the ferry were brought to orbit by winged spaceships. Expended space shuttle tanks are used as readymade structures for storage rather than being discarded, as they are now.* **Below:** *a future unmanned winged spaceship explores the surface of Mars by using its long wings to carry itself aloft in the thin Martian atmosphere.*

SPACE SHUTTLE FLIGHT STATISTICS

FLIGHT NUMBER	VEHICLE	DATES (LAUNCH TO LANDING)	FLIGHT TIME, LANDING SITE	NUMBER OF ORBITS	MISSION OBJECTIVES	CREW
STS-1	COLUMBIA	4/12/81 4/14/81	2d6h20m52s EAFB	36	Orbiter test program.	John Young, C Robert Crippen, P
STS-2	COLUMBIA	11/12/81 11/14/81	2d6h13m12s EAFB	36	Orbiter test program. RMS test. Earth study experiments.	Joseph Engle, C Richard Truly, P
STS-3	COLUMBIA	3/22/82 3/30/82	8d5m EAFB	129	Orbiter test program. Science experiments.	Jack Lousma, C Charles Fullerton, P
STS-4	COLUMBIA	6/27/82 7/ 4/82	7d1h9m39s EAFB	112	Orbiter test program. Science experiments. First Getaway Special.	Thomas Mattingly, C Henry Hartsfield, P
STS-5	COLUMBIA	11/11/82 11/16/82	5d2h14m25s EAFB	81	Launch ANIK C-3 and SBS-C satellites.	Vance Brand, C Robert Overmyer, P Joseph Allen, MS William Lenoir, MS
STS-6	CHALLENGER	4/ 4/83 4/ 9/83	5d24m32s EAFB	80	Tracking Data and Relay Satellite launched. First spacewalk.	Paul Weitz, C Karol Bobko, P Donald Peterson, MS Story Musgrave, MS
STS-7	CHALLENGER	6/18/83 6/24/83	6d2h24m10s EAFB	97	Launch ANIK C-2 and PALAPA B-1 satellites. Launch and retrieval of SPAS-1. First U.S. woman astronaut.	Robert Crippen, C Frederick Hauck, P John Fabian, MS Sally Ride, MS Norman Thagard, MS

FLIGHT NUMBER	VEHICLE	DATES (LAUNCH TO LANDING)	FLIGHT TIME, LANDING SITE	NUMBER OF ORBITS	MISSION OBJECTIVES	CREW
STS-8	CHALLENGER	8/30/83 9/ 5/83	6d1h8m40s EAFB	97	Launch of INSAT-1B satellite. Biology experiments. First black American astronaut. First night launch and night landing.	Richard Truly, C Daniel Brandenstein, P Dale Gardner, MS Guion Bluford, MS William Thornton, MS
STS-9	COLUMBIA	11/28/83 12/ 8/83	10d7h47m EAFB	167	Spacelab 1. First foreign astronaut on the shuttle.	John Young, C Brewster Shaw, P Owen Garriott, MS Robet Parker, MS Byron Lichtenberg, PS Ulf Merbold, PS
41-B	CHALLENGER	2/ 3/84 2/ 11/84	7d23h17m KSC	127	Launch WESTAR VI and PALAPA B-2 satellites. First MMU flights. SPAS launch and recovery. First landing at KSC.	Vance Brand, C Robert Gibson, P Bruce McCandless, MS Ronald McNair, MS Robert Stewart, MS
41-C	CHALLENGER	4/ 6/84 4/ 13/84	6d23h40m EAFB	108	Launch of Long Duration Exposure Facility. Rescue and repair of Solar Max.	Robert Crippen, C Francis Scobee, P George Nelson, MS James van Hoften, MS Terry Hart, MS
41-D	DISCOVERY	8/30/84 9/ 5/84	6d56m EAFB	97	Launch of LEASAT-2, SBS-4, and TELSTAR 3-C satellites. Extended 32 m solar panel.	Henry Hartsfield, C Michael Coats, P Judith Resnik, MS Richard Mullane, MS Steven Hawley, MS Charles Walker, PS

FLIGHT NUMBER	VEHICLE	DATES (LAUNCH TO LANDING)	FLIGHT TIME, LANDING SITE	NUMBER OF ORBITS	MISSION OBJECTIVES	CREW
41-G	CHALLENGER	10/ 5/84 10/13/84	8d5h23m KSC	133	Launch of Earth Radiation Budget satellite. Earth science experiments. Spacewalk to practice satellite refueling.	Robert Crippen, C Jon McBride, P David Leestma, MS Sally Ride, MS Kathryn Sullivan, MS Paul Scully-Power, PS Marc Garneau, PS
51-A	DISCOVERY	11/ 8/84 11/16/84	7d23h45m KSC	127	Launch of ANIK D-2 and LEASAT IV-1 satellites. Retreival of PALAPA B-2 and WESTAR VI satellites.	Frederick Hauck, C David Walker, P Anna Fisher, MS Joseph Allen, MS Dale Gardner, MS
51-C	DISCOVERY	1/24/85 1/27/85	3d1h33m KSC	DNR	Department of Defense mission. Objectives undisclosed.	Thomas Mattingly, C Loren Shriver, P James Buchli, MS Ellison Onizuka, MS Gary Payton, PS
51-D	DISCOVERY	4/12/85 4/19/85	6d23h55m20s KSC	110	Launch ANIK C-1 and LEASAT 3 satellites.	Karol Bobko, C Donald Williams, P Rhea Seddon, MS David Griggs, MS Jeffrey Hoffman, MS Charles D. Walker, MS Sen. Jake Garn, PS
51-B	CHALLENGER	4/29/85 5/ 6/85	7d8m EAFB	111	Spacelab 3. Biological and materials processing experiments.	Robert Overmyer, C Frederick Gregory, P Don Lind, MS Norman Thagard, MS William Thornton, MS Lodewijk van den Berg, PS Taylor Wang, PS

FLIGHT NUMBER	VEHICLE	DATES (LAUNCH TO LANDING)	FLIGHT TIME, LANDING SITE	NUMBER OF ORBITS	MISSION OBJECTIVES	CREW
51-G	DISCOVERY	6/17/85 6/24/85	7d1h38m53s EAFB	112	Launched MORELOS-1, ARABSAT 1-B, and TELSTAR 3-D satellites. Deployed and retrieved SPARTAN 1.	Daniel Brandenstein, C John Creighton, P Shannon Lucid, MS Steven Nagel, MS John Fabian, MS Patrick Baudry, PS Sultan Al-Saud, PS
51-F	CHALLENGER	7/29/85 8/ 6/85	7d22h45m26s EAFB	126	Spacelab 2 and 3 pallets. Life science and physics experiments.	Charles Fullerton, C Roy Bridges, P Story Musgrave, MS Anthony England, MS Karl Heinze, MS Loren Acton, PS John-David Bartoe, PS
51-5	DISCOVERY	8/27/85 9/ 3/85	7d2h18m29s EAFB	112	Launch AUSSAT-1, ASC-1, and LEASAT-4 satellites. Spacewalk to repair LEASAT-3 and redeploy.	Joe Engle, C Richard Covey, P James van Hoften, MS John Lounge, MS William Fisher, MS
51-J	ATLANTIS	10/ 3/85 10/ 7/85	4d1h45m EAFB	DNR	Department of Defense mission. Objectives undisclosed.	Karol Bobko, C Ronald Grabe, P Robert Stewart, MS David Hilmers, MS William Pailes, PS
61-A	CHALLENGER	10/30/85 11/ 6/85	7d44m51s EAFB	110	German Spacelab mission. Life and materials science, communications, and navigation experiments.	Henry Hartsfield, C Steven Nagel, P James Buchli, MS Guion Bluford, MS Bonnie Dunbar, MS Reinhard Furrer, PS Ernst Messerschmid, PS Wubbo Ockels, PS

FLIGHT NUMBER	VEHICLE	DATES (LAUNCH TO LANDING)	FLIGHT TIME, LANDING SITE	NUMBER OF ORBITS	MISSION OBJECTIVES	CREW
61-B	ATLANTIS	11/26/85 12/ 3/85	6d21h4m50s EAFB	108	Launch MORELOS-B, AUSSAT-2, and SATCOM KU-2 satellites. Spacewalk for structure-building experiments.	Brewster Shaw, C Bryan O'Connor, P Mary Cleave, MS Sherwood Spring, MS Jerry Ross, MS Rodolfo Neri Vela, PS Charles Walker, PS
61-C	COLUMBIA	1/12/86 1/18/86	6d2h4m9s KSC	96	Launch RCA SATCOM KU-1 satellite.	Robert Gibson, C Charles Bolden, P Franklin Chang-Diaz, MS Steven Hawley, MS George Nelson, MS Robert Cenker, PS Rep. Bill Nelson, PS
51-L	CHALLENGER	1/28/86*			Launch TDRS satellite. Spartan-Halley's Comet experiment. Teacher in Space.	Francis Scobee, C Michael Smith, P Judith Resnik, MS Ellison Onizuka, MS Ronald McNair, MS Christa McAuliffe, TISP Gregory Jarvis, PS

d	Day
h	Hour
m	Minute
s	Second
KSC	Landing at the Kennedy Space Center
EAFB	Landing at Edwards Air Force Base
C	Commander
P	Pilot
MS	Mission Specialist
PS	Payload Specialist
TISP	Teacher In Space
DNR	Details Not Released
*	Mission Unsuccessful

INDEX